The Faith to Flourish

Bible Lessons from the Olive Tree for a Rooted, Resilient, and Fruitful Life

Christine Caine

SEVEN-SESSION BIBLE STUDY GUIDE + STREAMING VIDEO

But I am like a flourishing olive tree in the house of God;
I trust in God's faithful love forever and ever.
PSALM 52:8

Faith to Flourish Bible Study Guide

Published under arrangement with HarperCollins Christian Resources, 3950 Sparks Drive SE, Suite 101, Grand Rapids, MI 49546, USA. HarperChristian Resources is a registered trademark of HarperCollins Christian Publishing, Inc.

Requests for information should be addressed to customercare@harpercollins.com.

HarperChristian Resources titles may be purchased in bulk for church, business, fundraising, or ministry use. For information, please email ResourceSpecialist@ChurchSource.com.

Published in association with Yates & Yates, www.yates2.com.

HarperCollins Publishers, Macken House, 39/40 Mayor Street Upper, Dublin 1, D01 C9W8, Ireland (https://www.harpercollins.com)

Art direction: Ron Huizinga

Second Printing June 2026 / Printed in the United States of America

Table of Contents

About the Author

Christine Caine is a speaker, activist, and *New York Times* bestselling author of *The Faith to Flourish*, who awakens people globally to discover their God-given purpose and live transformed lives for Jesus. Christine and her husband, Nick, have two daughters, Catherine and Sophia. Together, Christine and Nick founded A21, a global anti-human trafficking organization that prevents exploitation, recovers victims, and empowers survivors to rebuild their lives. She also founded Propel Women, an initiative that activates women to follow Jesus wholeheartedly and live confidently in their calling. You can tune into Christine's Equip & Empower podcast for practical insights and encouragement, drawing hope from Jesus wherever you are. To learn more about Christine and her resources, visit christinecaine.com.

How to Use This Study

The Faith to Flourish Bible Study Guide includes two major parts: *Group Study* and *Personal Study*. Both are essential to meaningful time with God and the people in your group.

GROUP STUDY

Gathering regularly with other Christians in encouragement and provocation of love and good works is vital to everyone's flourishing (Hebrews 10:25). This is an environment for worshiping God together over a specified period of time in His Word. Commitment to your group includes showing up, being present, prepared, and contributing to the conversation. The Group Study includes four components:

Watch

Use the outline provided for taking notes during the video teaching.

Discuss

Carefully written questions and comments are provided each week to engage the teaching content and concepts deeper together as a group. If you do not have a specified group leader, take turns reading the set up and prompts aloud to the group.

Feel free to follow the Spirit, using any of the recommended questions that fit naturally into your conversation, skipping any that don't, and adding comments or questions of your own to facilitate a meaningful interaction with the material and with other group members.

Grow

Within the discussion guide, questions for deeper reflection and application are provided. The goal of this study is spiritual growth, not just in knowledge but in life. If time is limited, don't skip this important part of the Group Study. We cannot flourish without putting into practice the things we are learning.

Pray

Open and close your Group Study with prayer. Before watching the video, simply ask the Spirit to open your hearts and minds to what God's Word has to say to you during your time together. A suggested prayer is provided to conclude your time together.

TEACHING VIDEOS

Streaming video access is included with this study. Access instructions are printed on the inside cover of your guide.

Each week has essential teaching for the group session. Most groups will choose to watch the teaching videos at the beginning of their time together. However, it is an option to watch the videos before gathering, allowing more time for discussion. Either way, the videos are a vital part of this discipleship resource.

PERSONAL STUDY

Another vital part of a flourishing Christian life is the steady rhythm of daily devotion. This resource includes five days of content to be completed individually between times together as a group. Each week includes four days of study and one day of reflection—both formats are designed to take around thirty minutes to complete:

Days 1–4 include reading, questions or prompts, and a prayer. These days are more robust than what you may find in something like a typical devotional. The daily studies take you deeper into the weekly themes.

Day 5 is unique. You'll conclude the week with a day of guided prayer and journaling.

DISCIPLESHIP EXPERIENCE: WEEK 7

Finally, it's important to note that the final week of this study is unique, concluding your time together with a prayer experience.

You will share a meal together in your final gathering. This time will be full of olive-inspired dishes as well as food and drink to pair with them. Plan for everyone to provide something for this fun time of fellowship.

Another way to enhance this final experience is to exchange recipes. Inspiration and instructions can be found on page 221.

Eating together is a key part of this experience, much like sharing a meal was an act of deep fellowship in biblical times, but the emphasis will be on prayer.

Introduction

Only the sea itself seems as ancient a part of the region as the olive and its oil that, like no other products of nature, have shaped civilizations from remotest antiquity to the present.
LAWRENCE DURRELL, PROSPERO'S CELL

"And here, on the west side of the Erechtheion, we have the ruins of the Pandroseion. There would have been a wall to our left and an entrance about where we're standing. And directly in front of us is the sacred olive tree . . ."

It was the summer of 2022, and I was standing in the ruins of the sanctuary for Pandrosus high atop the Acropolis where I'd taken a group of friends, and together we were listening to our tour guide. Well, at least all my friends were. I'll admit, after the first hour, and it not being my first time to climb the Acropolis, I was starting to fade. Still, being Greek and being in Greece, I wanted my friends to experience the most Greek thing Greece has going—the Parthenon.

Growing up in a big, crazy, Greek family in Australia, we had images of the Parthenon all throughout our home. I daresay Mum had a replica of it on the end of the mantle that never moved, not even when baby Jesus and the entire nativity set was brought out at Christmas and sprawled across it. Of course, I would choose Jesus over the Parthenon any day, but as a child, I never would have suggested we move Mum's replica or any of the other Greek icons scattered throughout our house paying homage to the homeland and its ancient treasures.

Designed twenty-five centuries ago, the Parthenon stands tall against a sky that's often as blue as the Greek flag—or the Aegean Sea—both of which are breathtaking to me. Though constructed between 447 BC and 438 BC as a celebration of the Hellenic victory over Persian invaders during the Greco-Persian Wars, it has always served as a temple dedicated to the goddess Athena Parthenos—the namesake for the city of Athens.[1] To architects throughout history, the Parthenon has been called the most perfect building ever built. Though it survived the first 600 years in its original state, it went on to see 3400 years of conquests, bombings, reconstructions, and preservation work. [2]

But none of its classical architecture captured my attention that day. What left me in awe was the sacred olive tree. I had been coming to the Acropolis for decades, since my first trip to Greece in 1987, and never had I really paid attention to the sacred olive tree. You certainly can't miss it once you're at the top. Amidst a sea of sand-colored marble, stones, pebbled walkways, and ruins, it stands green, vibrant, and flourishing. And yet, somehow, I'd missed it.

Wandering over to the information plaque, I found myself absorbed in reading about the sacred olive tree. According to Greek mythology, the tree was a gift from Athena herself. When she and Poseidon competed for the patronage of the city, she struck the ground with her spear, and the initial sprig of the olive tree sprouted.[3] Of course, the tree that had me mesmerized was not that tree, but as legend has it, every tree that has stood there can be traced back to the original tree. In fact, the most recent planting was placed there by the American School of Archaeology in 1952, after they saved and harvested a four-foot branch from the previous tree that endured destruction during World War II.[4]

What resilience. What strength. What extraordinary ability to not only survive and grow but to thrive and flourish. All alone. Atop one of the highest points in Athens. I have always loved olives, olive oil, and everything made from olive oil, and though I love olive trees and have two in my front yard, never had I been more captivated than I was in that moment. With one tree. And never had I felt God nudging me to study a tree. The olive tree.

Once I was back home, I began to read everything I could find about olive trees—their fruit, the products made from their wood, their enemies, their medicinal properties, and how to grow and care for them. I sought to settle, once and for all, their origin, secretly hoping they really did originate in Greece. Of course, that's what I'll always believe, but no doubt the Spaniards and the Italians will argue the point.

I was amazed at all I learned. Did you know there is a World Olive Tree Day? It takes place November 26. Who knew? And did you know that Olive trees have been depicted in art throughout history? They've been the subjects of Claude Monet, Henri Matisse, and Salvador Dali. One of my favorite works of art is *Olive Grove*, part of a series of olive tree paintings by Van Gogh from 1889. I found references to olive trees in poetry, songs, movies, and historical writings. In *The Odyssey*, an ancient poem attributed to Homer, the description of two olive trees is used to convey a sense of reassurance, letting the reader know of the legendary Greek King Odysseus' safety.[5] I found songs from the 1960s, and films about justice and political films using the olive tree as symbolism throughout. I even found a made-for-tv rom-com called *Love Under the Olive Tree* that's all about olive oil making. I'm not saying I watched it all the way through, but I was amazed at all the ways olive trees have been depicted in the arts—and I love olive oil. I often joke, but I don't doubt it for a minute, that Mum put it in my baby bottle. After all, we were Greek! I remember Mum adding it to recipes, rubbing it on her hands, coating squeaky hinges, and dousing our salads, cheese, and bread with it. Thanks to Mum, we ate olive oil in everything and on everything. I'm sure her obsession with olive oil is why, to this day, I can't get enough.

Included in my vast research was every biblical reference to olive trees, olive oil, olive branches, and olive anything. To my delight, there were plenty! I found that God obviously likes olives and olive trees, and not just because He made them. Together, we are going to discover the beauty, grace, strength, and importance of the olive tree, and its relevance in our lives. We are called to thrive and flourish in every season of life, to be resilient, strong, and able to endure—all qualities we'll discover in our study of the olive tree.

I'm excited to dive into Scripture with you and uncover the deep truths hidden in the olive tree. After this study, you will never look at another olive tree the same way again. Let's get started!

Love,

WEEK 1

Rooted in God's Presence

GROUP STUDY

Watch

Watch the video for Week 1: Rooted in God's Presence, recording your thoughts as you listen. Access instructions are printed on the inside cover of your guide.

How do we not just survive, but truly flourish, when life feels chaotic and difficult?

> *But I am like a green olive tree in the house of God. I trust in the steadfast love of God forever and ever.*
> PSALM 52:8 ESV

To understand David's declaration, we must first understand his circumstances.

David's life demonstrates that it is possible to experience outer chaos without inner chaos when we are rooted in Christ.

David didn't choose the olive tree by accident. It is a profound symbol of life, resilience, and divine intimacy.

We are called to be like the olive tree—resilient, fruitful, and beautiful in God's house.

Flourishing isn't about our strength; it's about the object of our trust—God's faithful love.

Our trust in God's future faithfulness is built on our gratitude for His past faithfulness.

KEY CHARACTERISTICS OF THE OLIVE TREE

- RESILIENCE AND ENDURANCE
- FRUITFULNESS
- LONGEVITY
- BEAUTY AND DIGNITY

Discuss

Leader (or volunteer), read the following aloud to the group and follow with the prompts for discussion.

In Psalm 52, David declares, "But I am like a green olive tree in the house of God. I trust in the steadfast love of God forever and ever" (ESV).

David wrote these verses when he was on the run, being slandered, lied about, mocked, and laughed at. He was hiding in caves because Saul wanted to kill him. Yet, in the midst of affliction, he saw himself as an olive tree.

In the Bible, the olive tree symbolizes life. Though not tall or stately, olive trees are long-lived, dependable, and resilient. They display permanence and endurance while flourishing in the worst conditions. In fact, the word *green* in verse 8 is also translated as "flourishing" in other translations.

> **Select a volunteer to read Psalm 52:4–9 aloud.**
>
> *You love any words that destroy, you treacherous tongue!*
>
> *This is why God will bring you down forever. He will take you, ripping you out of your tent; he will uproot you from the land of the living. Selah*
>
> *The righteous will see and fear, and they will derisively say about that hero, "Here is the man who would not make God his refuge, but trusted in the abundance of his riches, taking refuge in his destructive behavior."*
>
> *But I am like a flourishing olive tree in the house of God; I trust in God's faithful love forever and ever. I will praise you forever for what you have done. In the presence of your faithful people, I will put my hope in your name, for it is good.*
> PSALM 52:4–9

Pause for a moment and look over your notes. Though few of us will ever experience the physical danger David was in when he wrote Psalm 52, I imagine that we can relate to the chaos in his life. There is no doubt that every one of us has experienced times of disappointment, disillusionment, discouragement, betrayal, loss, grief, being falsely accused, misunderstood, or traumatic seasons of pain and suffering, be it mentally, emotionally, or physically. Such pain leaves us feeling demoralized, deflated and depleted, doesn't it?

Is there anything going on in your life now, or in your sphere of influence, that you would label as chaos? Describe how it makes you feel.

Before this study, what did the imagery of an olive tree bring to your mind? How has the teaching deepened or changed your understanding of what it means to be a "green olive tree"?

David shows that in Christ we can experience outer chaos without having inner chaos. Has this been true for you? Explain your understanding of this in your own words.

The olive tree is a powerful symbol of **resilience**, **endurance**, and **longevity**. It is designed to thrive in harsh conditions and regenerate even after being cut down.

Which of these characteristics—resilience, endurance, or longevity—do you most desire in your spiritual life right now, and why?

Read Colossians 2:6–7. How does being "rooted and built up in him" give us the strength to endure seasons of hardship, much like the root system of an olive tree?

When David said he was like a green olive tree, his deliverance was still in his future. But he was so confident that he was already singing his future thankfulness. David knew God would deliver him because He had done it before. Trust in God's future faithfulness is rooted in gratitude for God's past faithfulness.

How has God been faithful to you in the past? How has He delivered, healed, led, or provided for you?

We, too, can be like a green olive tree in the house of God. We can flourish in difficult circumstances if we remain in the presence of God. We can trust in God's faithful love forever.

GROW

Consider these questions as they relate to what you've seen and heard today.

David didn't just see himself as an olive tree, but as an olive tree "in the house of God" (Psalm 52:8). This positioning implies protection, belonging, and intimacy. What practical steps can we take this week to intentionally position ourselves "in the house of God"—to draw nearer to His presence and community—especially when we feel overwhelmed by the world outside?

In what tangible ways can we remind each other this week that, through Christ, we are created to flourish, not just survive?

PRAY

Leader (or volunteer) read the prayer aloud, or pray independently over your group before closing your time together.

Father, I'm so grateful that You have made me to be like a green olive tree, able to thrive in every season of life. Help me remember that You are always with me. Give me the courage and strength to continually praise You all the days of my life. In Jesus' name, amen.

WEEK 1 | Rooted in God's Presence

PERSONAL STUDY

The steady rhythm of daily devotion is a vital part of flourishing in your life with Jesus. Set aside time this week to really dig into God's Word. Each day, open yourself up to the Spirit's work in your heart and mind. Then, prayerfully reflect on the beautiful truth He is revealing during this season of new growth.

DAY 1
Rooted and Resilient

DAY 2
Strong and Sturdy

DAY 3
Shelter and Protection

DAY 4
Beautiful to Behold

DAY 5
Guided Prayer and Journaling

DAY 1 Rooted and Resilient

Sitting down to a table outside a restaurant in Riomaggiore, all Nick and I wanted to do was celebrate. I had just crossed off one of the things on my bucket list. For as long as I remember, I wanted to hike the Cinque Terre Trail in Northern Italy, and today, we did it—and all in one day!

The trail was full of twists and turns that hugged the seaside cliffs. At times it involved climbing up hewn steps carved out of the rocky mountainside or carefully working our way down a steep and rocky hillside. At other times we traversed ancient stone foot paths or newly built ones made of wood jutting out over jagged rocks and crashing waves—all of it breathtaking.

At one point during our hike, I walked under a canopy of olive trees planted on each side of the path, one right after the other. Because it was after I had seen the Sacred Olive Tree at the Parthenon and begun to research this study, I couldn't help but stop and admire them. I wanted to take in every facet of them. I touched the leaves. I rubbed the bark. I closed my eyes and inhaled. Though all the fruit had already been harvested, in my imagination I still could smell them.

Still taking them all in, I watched as the breeze tossed their limbs and the sunlight danced on their silvery leaves. What I marveled at most was how they clung to the terraces while reaching for the sky. It was then I began to imagine what all was underground holding them in place.

Olive trees have two kinds of roots for every tree. First, a thick, strong taproot goes straight down and deep. Second, thinner shallow roots span out in every direction going as far out as twice the width of the canopy of the tree. The taproot is strong and anchors the tree to the earth, while the shallow roots running wide in the topsoil act as a stabilizing force. And both draw all the water and nutrients the tree needs to grow. Because of their root system, olive trees can flourish in dry places. If the roots are well established, then they are resistant to drought and can go long periods of time, months even, without rain.[1]

The root system is so robust that it's capable of regenerating itself even when the aboveground structure of the tree is destroyed by frost, fire, or disease. In 1985, in Tuscany, "a severe frost destroyed many productive and aged olive trees, ruining the livelihoods of many farmers. However, when new shoots appeared in the spring and the dead wood was removed, they . . . became new fruit-producing trees."[2] What's more, even withstanding such dire circumstances, they can live for hundreds of years—all because of their hardy root system.[3]

An olive tree with strong roots grows green and bears olives. Similarly, when we are rooted, we bear fruit spiritually. Thinking on all this, if we're olive trees, what are our roots supposed to be like, spiritually speaking? What would it mean for us to have a taproot? And then some shallow roots running the left of us, the right of us, behind us, and before us? How do we grow a spiritual root system that's as resilient as an olive tree's physical root system, so that we too can endure the inevitable storms, challenges, trials, and tribulations of life?

> *So then, just as you received Christ Jesus as Lord, continue to walk in him, being rooted and built up in him and established in the faith, just as you were taught, and overflowing with gratitude.*
>
> COLOSSIANS 2:6–7

To begin answering such questions, let's examine the different ways the Bible speaks about roots. Read the following verses and circle the word *root*.

"Be sure there is no man, woman, clan, or tribe among you today whose heart turns away from the LORD our God to go and worship the gods of those nations. Be sure there is no root among you bearing poisonous and bitter fruit."

DEUTERONOMY 29:18

On that day the root of Jesse will stand as a banner for the peoples. The nations will look to him for guidance, and his resting place will be glorious.

ISAIAH 11:10

For the love of money is a root of all kinds of evil, and by craving it, some have wandered away from the faith and pierced themselves with many griefs.

1 TIMOTHY 6:10

Make sure that no one falls short of the grace of God and that no root of bitterness springs up, causing trouble and defiling many.

HEBREWS 12:15

Now, next to each verse, explain what or who the word *root* refers to.

The verb form of *root* is "rooted, rooting, or roots."[4] When we plant anything, we start by rooting it. We might put in a small container as a seedling and set it under a light. We might mist it and try to recreate the optimal conditions for it to grow. Our objective is for it to root—to take hold—and grow more roots. When it does, and anchors itself in the ground, we say it's rooted.[5]

To be rooted in something is to be "firmly implanted."[6] In our spiritual lives, in order to grow and mature in Christ, we need to be rooted in Christ. Look up Colossians 2:6–7 and record your findings.

When an olive tree has strong and healthy roots, it appears above ground as a green, flourishing tree that bears a crop of olives. Similarly, it is only when we are rooted that we bear fruit spiritually.

What thoughts or feelings do you have about what Jesus says about fruit below?

> *"My Father is glorified by this: that you produce much fruit and prove to be my disciples."*
> JOHN 15:8

Growth, maturity, and fruit require strong roots in Jesus. Without them, we would starve of the nutrients we need to grow in Christ, unable to stand firm during the storms of life.

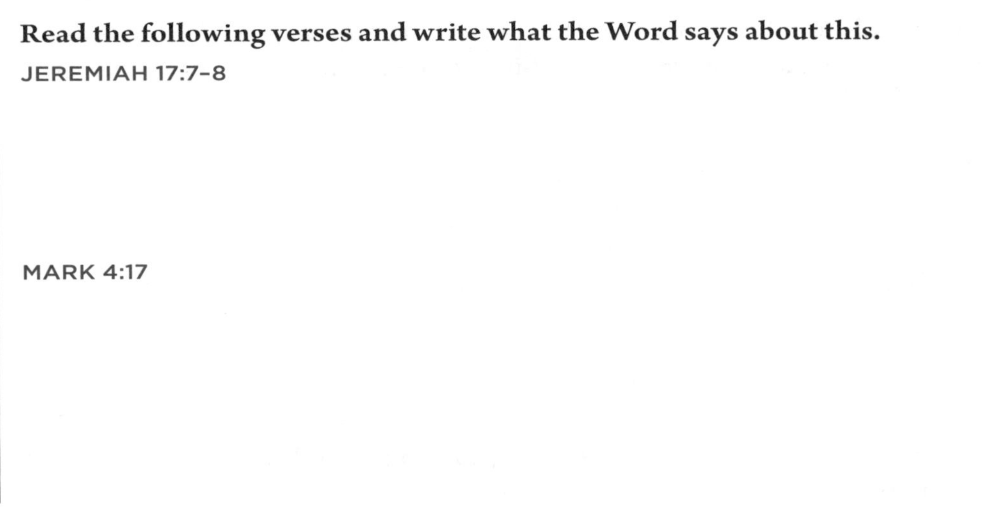

Read the following verses and write what the Word says about this.

JEREMIAH 17:7–8

MARK 4:17

With all of this in mind, even as we grow deep spiritual roots, at times we must uproot what is not producing good fruit in our lives (Ecclesiastes 3:1–2). Jeremiah confirms there are times "to uproot and tear down, to destroy and overthrow, to build and to plant" (Jeremiah 1:10 NIV).

In my life, I experienced major trauma as a result of being abandoned at birth, adopted, sexually abused, and marginalized because of my ethnicity. I had to uproot deeply painful things that controlled my life for years—things like shame, rejection, fear, bitterness, offense, and insecurity. I also had to deal with the fruit of those roots in my life by renewing my mind according to the Word, working with a Christian counselor, and learning new patterns of behavior. None of it happened over night, but over the course of years.

Are there painful roots that you've pulled up? What were they and how did you pull them up?

There will probably always be more that needs uprooted in you because Jesus never stops healing us. What are some things that still need to be uprooted in your life?

Ask God to help you identify your part in uprooting such things, and write your thoughts here.

Hebrews 12:15 commands us to "make sure" that no wrong root of bitterness springs up. This principle and practice of *making sure* applies to any wrong root.

Take a few minutes to reflect. How can we make sure that the wrong roots aren't growing?

Being rooted in Christ and strengthening our roots, we become resilient like the olive tree. We can grow and thrive, even in the hard places. We can flourish in every season of life. So, let's keep going and learn more about why David said he was like an olive tree!

PRAY

Leader (or volunteer) read the prayer aloud, or pray independently over your group before closing your time together.

My prayer for you today is based in Ephesians 3:16–19.

I pray that He may grant you, according to the riches of His glory, to be strengthened with power in your inner being through His Spirit, and that Christ may dwell in your hearts through faith. I pray that you, being rooted and firmly established in love, may be able to comprehend with all the saints what is the length and width, height and depth of God's love, and to know Christ's love that surpasses knowledge, so that you may be filled with all the fullness of God.

DAY 2 Strong and Sturdy

When my girls were younger, someone gave our family season passes to Disneyland. For a year, we would go as often as our schedules allowed so the girls could have a bit of fun. For Sophia, my youngest, the wait times in line were excruciating. Like any child, she'd grow restless and then she'd say her feet hurt, or she had to go to the bathroom . . . again. No one likes waiting in lines of any kind. Not at the supermarket, in a department store, at a concert, or at the movies, but that is the way life is sometimes. Of course, once our wait is over and we get through the line, we quickly forget all our discomfort.

I remember somewhere in that season of life we discovered that Disney offered a way to short circuit the long waits. It was a complimentary service called FastPass where you could make reservations and skip to the front of the line. They've since done away with FastPass, but for two girls who grew up in the age of instant access to most everything, it felt miraculous!

No doubt, we live in a world that feels like it moves faster and faster every day; and for the most part, we want it this way, don't we? We live in an instant-gratification world where we can google anything and have answers in minutes. We can snap a picture and upload it to social media within seconds and make it instantly available to everyone in the world. We can order something online and have it delivered in the same day. But not everything in this life was meant to happen quickly. Some things were designed to take time . . . for our good.

I found this to be true more than ever in my study of the olive tree because one of the distinct characteristics of the olive tree is that it grows at a snail's pace. It is not a fast-growing tree at all. If you plant a grove of olive trees, all in hopes of developing a profitable olive farm, then you better prepare yourself to wait a number of years. In fact, it can take as many as ten years for an olive tree to ever begin producing olives.

While an olive tree is growing from one year to the next before it ever produces the first olive, a lot of growth you can't see is happening—and it's more of what makes the olive tree strong and sturdy. Years of slow steady growth make the olive tree's wood some of the most tightly grained and dense in the world. The consistent slow pace of growing makes the wood not only hard, but also dry, and therefore highly appreciated by woodcrafters. In fact, on the Janka hardness scale, olive wood is harder than oak.[1] It's no wonder that it has been used since ancient times to craft and build so many things. It's rich caramel color and straight grain, along with its fruity scent, has attracted artisans for centuries. In my travels I've discovered everything from furniture to kitchen utensils to fruit bowls to chess sets to nativity carvings. I found that it's not often harvested for lumber, as the trunks can grow twisted, but the wood itself is still highly sought after.[2]

With all this in mind, note what olive trees are used for in the following verses.

1 KINGS 6:23, 31–33

NEHEMIAH 8:15

We know from Scripture that Jesus entered this earth as a newborn babe, and that He grew. God designed our lives to begin in this way, didn't He? Everything starts as a seed—including us—and seeds take time to grow. None of us can fast track our growth process—not physically or spiritually.

While we know Jesus came into this world as a baby, what we don't know in great detail is what His life was like on a daily basis, as He grew—as a toddler, as a little boy, as a preteen and then a teen, and as a young man. We know He preached in the temple when He was twelve (Luke 2:41–50) and we know He started His earthly ministry at age thirty (Luke 3:23).

Jesus couldn't have leapfrogged from being a preteen to adulthood, so how did He grow between the ages of twelve and thirty? He obviously didn't skip eighteen years of His life. Read the following verses and list the ways the Bible says Jesus grew.

LUKE 2:40, 52

I love how Luke wrote that Jesus "grew up." Isn't that what we're supposed to do? Not only physically, but spiritually, mentally, emotionally, intellectually, relationally, socially, and financially? We're called to mature, which is what the Bible calls our growing process.

In Greek, the word *grew* comes from the same root word as *increase.* It is used to measure many things, including the maturation process.[3] Jesus matured. He increased. He grew internally while He was growing externally. We might easily glaze over how Jesus matured, especially if we're familiar with these verses from Luke, but I don't want us to miss the depth of what God has for us.

Read the following definitions of *wisdom, stature,* and *favor,* and then answer the questions that follow. I want us to see what they can teach us about growing strong and sturdy like an olive tree.

Wisdom is "knowledge," "insight," "good sense," "judgment," and "the ability to discern qualities and relationships."[4] "Perhaps [it] connotes the practical side of Jesus' teaching, so simple and direct, but it could also include a deeper knowledge of mission and God's purpose of salvation." Ultimately, God revealed His wisdom in the person of Jesus Christ (1 Corinthians 1:24, 30).[5]

Stature "usually refers to the height of a person, sometimes figuratively (Ezek. 17:6; 19:11). . . . It was used to show the weakness of humanity and the need to rely on God (Matt. 6:27; Luke 12:25). It was also used as a measure of the maturity of the Christian (Eph. 4:13)."[6]

Favor is "gaining approval, acceptance, or special benefits. . . . There is also a close association between favor, grace, and mercy, which are sometimes used to translate the same Hebrew and Greek words (such as *hēn* and *charis*). . . . [Favor with] God depends on his good pleasure and is often extended in response to prayer or righteous living (Gen. 6:8; Ex. 33:12–13)".[7]

Considering these definitions, can you think of ways you can grow in wisdom, stature, and favor?

WISDOM	STATURE	FAVOR

There's something else I don't want us to miss from Luke 2:52—Jesus kept growing; He didn't stop. He kept a posture of growth.

Read and reflect on the following verses. Circle any words that stand out to you about how we remain in a posture of growth.

But speaking the truth in love, let us grow in every way into him who is the head—Christ. From him the whole body, fitted and knit together by every supporting ligament, promotes the growth of the body for building itself up in love by the proper working of each individual part.
EPHESIANS 4:15–16

Although by this time you ought to be teachers, you need someone to teach you the basic principles of God's revelation again. You need milk, not solid food. Now everyone who lives on milk is inexperienced with the message about righteousness, because he is an infant. But solid food is for the mature—for those whose senses have been trained to distinguish between good and evil.
HEBREWS 5:12–14

Therefore, let us leave the elementary teaching about Christ and go on to maturity, not laying again a foundation of repentance from dead works, faith in God, teaching about ritual washings, laying on of hands, the resurrection of the dead, and eternal judgment.
HEBREWS 6:1–2

If you were to summarize all these verses, what would you say is our role in our personal growth?

When I gave my life fully to God, I began growing. I worshiped in community—in church. I read the Bible. I memorized verses to renew my mind. I prayed and kept a notebook of my answered prayers. I kept a journal of what I was learning, thinking, and desiring. All of that made me feel closer to God and encounter Him.

What spiritual disciplines do you practice to keep yourself growing in Christ? Put a star by any from this list that you practice consistently.

Daily Bible reading

Prayer

Worship

Times of silence and solitude

Honoring a Sabbath

Being a part of a healthy local church community

Expressing generosity

Participating in acts of service

We must recognize that we have an active role in our growth while we also know that God doesn't leave us on our own to grow. (If you want to *dig deeper*, consider the next few verses about how God works to help us grow: Philippians 2:13; John 14:26; Galatians 5:22–23.)

Growth in God is good, so good, and He is helping us. But as good as growth is, that doesn't make it easy.

In fact, the truth is that growing is rarely easy, as it often involves a bit of pain. I remember when Catherine was a preteen, and she would complain of her shins hurting or her hips aching. It was because she was growing. She was experiencing what we call growing pains.

Sometimes we feel something similar in our spiritual walk, don't we? It typically hurts to grow because growing involves stretching our spiritual muscles. It involves doing what we have never done before or going where we've never gone before. It involves trusting God when we'd rather avoid anything that feels like another risk—especially after we've been wounded, experienced trauma, been rejected, disappointed, disillusioned, or blindsided by something that hurts us deeply.

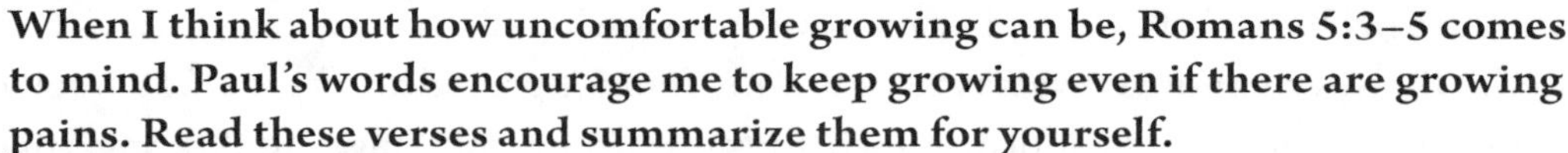

When I think about how uncomfortable growing can be, Romans 5:3–5 comes to mind. Paul's words encourage me to keep growing even if there are growing pains. Read these verses and summarize them for yourself.

I have consistently found that we need to grow to where we need to go, and slow growth produces the character we need to get there. Our character is the backbone of our purpose. So, even when it's uncomfortable, let's commit to practicing our spiritual disciplines—growing slowly, consistently, and intentionally. Let's be like the olive trees God has called us to be!

PRAY

Leader (or volunteer) read the prayer aloud, or pray independently over your group before closing your time together.

My prayer for you today is a declaration based on 2 Peter 1:3–9, that you may keep growing in your faith just as steadily as an olive tree.

His divine power has given you everything required for life and godliness through the knowledge of Him who called us by His own glory and goodness. By these He has given you great and precious promises, so that through them you may share in the divine nature, escaping the corruption that is in the world because of evil desire. For this very reason, make every effort to supplement your faith with goodness, goodness with knowledge, knowledge with self-control, self-control with endurance, endurance with godliness, godliness with brotherly affection, and brotherly affection with love. For if you possess these qualities in increasing measure, they will keep you from being useless or unfruitful in the knowledge of our Lord Jesus Christ. In Jesus' name, amen.

DAY 3 Shelter and Protection

Carrying a lawn chair out to our front yard, I picked a spot to sit where I could fully take in the front entrance to our home. I wanted to change it up a bit and thought staring at it might inspire me as to what we could do differently. I actually liked it the way it was, but sometimes change feels refreshing to me. Before I could get lost in imagining a new front door surrounded by bougainvillea or jasmine, two squirrels scampering across our lawn captured my attention. Chirping and squealing, they were chasing one another from one tree to the next. When they leaped onto the trunk of one of our olive trees and began going round and round it in an upward spiral, I couldn't help but laugh. To them this spring ritual was serious business, but to me, it was sheer entertainment. The more I watched them, the more fascinated I became. They never seemed to tire, and they never took their eyes off their opponent. With their tails ever twitching, they did pause here and there, maybe to catch their breath or to taunt one another more, but they were always ready to take off again in the flash of a second. As they ascended up the olive tree once more and disappeared into the top of the canopy, I began to think of how our two olive trees not only provided shade for me, but they were a safe haven for birds, squirrels, and who knows how many insects and bacteria and microorganisms that I knew nothing about. To my naked eye, they are beautiful trees I can never get enough of, but to migrating birds and squirrels and other critters too small for me to see, they are a world of biodiversity.

All around the world, olive groves and the environment where they are grown foster an ecosystem where a number of species coexist. Studies have determined that olive farms "can support up to 200 wild plant species, 90 vertebrates and 160 invertebrates species per" every two and a half acres.[1] Can you imagine? Many flora and fauna species depend on olive groves. From quail to partridges to sparrows to hoopoe, birds build their nests in the trees and take from them food for their survival. Squirrels and lizards are equally at home, as are raccoons who thoroughly enjoy eating olives.[2] While we may look at a grove of olive trees and only see trees and olives, there is an entire ecosystem being supported, sheltered, and protected by the trees.

What's more, a grove of olive trees can not only support an entire ecosystem, it "plays an essential role in the fight against climate change and desertification."[3] I know you don't want a science lesson, so let me just say that in the same way God created an olive tree to provide shelter, protection and safety for animals, He created us for community so we could experience the same—and then offer that same security to one another.

Let's start with understanding how God protects us. Write out the following verses and meditate on what these promises mean for you.

PSALM 46:1

NAHUM 1:7

Psalm 91 speaks of God's protection as both rescue from and refuge in the midst of attack. I have turned here over and over when I have felt bombarded by the attacks of the enemy. We can forget that we are in a spiritual battle when life is easy and comfortable, but one phone call or incident can quickly remind us of a very real enemy.

Write out the following verse that shows us who our adversary really is.

1 PETER 5:8

I have had to lean in to the protection and shelter of God when Nick and I received a text from Sophia's school telling us there was an active shooter in the area. I have had a phone call from the doctor telling me the test results had returned with a cancer diagnosis. I have experienced paralyzing fear and anxiety over unexpected betrayals, accusations, and heartache. I could spend all of today's study giving examples of times where I not only read and prayed Psalm 91 but slept with my Bible on my nightstand laying open to Psalm 91, all because I knew I needed God's supernatural protection in my life.

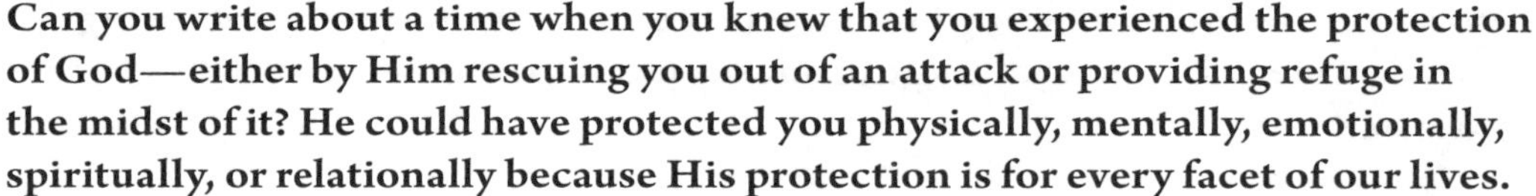

Can you write about a time when you knew that you experienced the protection of God—either by Him rescuing you out of an attack or providing refuge in the midst of it? He could have protected you physically, mentally, emotionally, spiritually, or relationally because His protection is for every facet of our lives.

How did it make you feel to know He was looking out for you?

We all prefer to be rescued from any attack, but *refuge* is protection, too. An olive tree provides shade from the sun in the heat of the day. Shade is defined as "shelter."[4] Have you ever been outside when a storm seemingly came out of nowhere and drenched you? Didn't you run for shelter right away? And didn't it provide protection?

The first verse of Psalm 91 says, "The one who lives under the protection of the Most High dwells in the shadow of the Almighty."

I take comfort in knowing that when the spiritual "heat" beats down on me, I can run to the shelter of the Most High. I can take refuge in His shade by dwelling in His shadow and being covered under His wings (Psalm 91:1, 4).

When I need to run for shelter, I often run to . . .

- The Word of God
- The People of God
- The House of God
- The Worship of God
- The Place of Prayer with God

How has God provided protection when you have run to the Word of God for shelter?

How has your community in Jesus helped when you have run to them for shelter?

God has called us to be like olive trees. Olive trees provide shelter for plants and animals, and we can provide shelter for others by being generous, a source of comfort, and as we help them learn how to rest in God's care.

How does God want to use you, as a Christ follower, to provide shelter for others this week? Before answering, read the following verses.

> *Everyone should look not to his own interests, but rather to the interests of others.*
> PHILIPPIANS 2:4
>
> *Therefore encourage one another and build each other up as you are already doing.*
> 1 THESSALONIANS 5:11
>
> *And let us consider one another in order to provoke love and good works, not neglecting to gather together, as some are in the habit of doing, but encouraging each other, and all the more as you see the day approaching.*
> HEBREWS 10:24–25

Through the years, I have had the privilege of hearing, comforting, and encouraging many of my sisters in Christ. One of the ways I've found it important to protect, to offer shelter, and to provide safety is to keep each person's confidence. Another way is by speaking God's truth, God's encouragement, to them. The next time someone comes to you seeking such shelter, be the olive tree that they need. Be the place of shelter and protection to them that God is to you.

PRAY

Leader (or volunteer) read the prayer aloud, or pray independently over your group before closing your time together.

As we close our time together, I want to encourage you to run to God, the Most High, and take refuge in His protection. As I do, I am praying parts of Psalm 91 over you. Will you pray with me?

Heavenly Father, as olive trees, we choose to live under the protection of You, the Most High. We dwell in the shadow of You, the Almighty. We say concerning You, the Lord, that You are our refuge and our fortress, our God in whom we trust. Because You have Your heart set on us, we know You will deliver us. You will protect us because You know our names. When You call out to us today, we will answer You. We trust that You will be with us in any trouble. You will rescue us and give us honor. You will satisfy us with long life and show us Your salvation. You will help us be a source of protection for others. In Jesus' name we pray, amen.

DAY 4 Beautiful to Behold

Closing my eyes and taking a deep breath, I did my best to inhale as much of the sweet smell of the olive tree blossoms as I could. With their licorice-like floral scent, they saturated the countryside. Nick and I were in Spain with our girls and had taken a day trip to the countryside so I could see the trees in bloom.

When we stepped in the grove and began walking through the trees, the fragrance was so strong, it was all I could smell—and it was then that I could see the blooms up close. They were utterly breathtaking. When I asked the farmer if all olive trees made such beautiful flowers, he said yes, but reminded me that there are as many five hundred cultivars of olive trees and that not all flowers look the same. David wrote, "I am like a flourishing olive tree in the house of God" (Psalm 52:8), but he didn't specify which cultivar of olive tree he was. How did he know what kind of olive tree to be like?

In a world with as many as five hundred cultivars, God said be like an olive tree, but he didn't specify for David or you or me to be like an Arbequina, Coratina, or a Picholine. He didn't say to be a Kalamata, Manzanilla, or Amfissa. He didn't say to be a Gordal Sevillano, Mission, or Nicoise. He just said for me—and you—to be like an olive tree.

All olive trees are beautiful, but if you look closely, one cultivar's beauty is different from another's. And yet, at their core, they are all beautiful to behold. Some trees are young, less than five years old and not even flowering yet. Some are a little older, just reaching eight or ten years old and producing fruit for the very first time. Some grow tall, racing toward the sky with straight trunks. Some grow to a certain height and stop, never to be taller than you or me. And some grow to be twiggy bushes.

What's more, every varietal's leaves are different. Yes, they are green, but some leaves at the top of a tree are lighter than ones at the bottom of a tree.[1] Some are silvery green year-round. When it comes to shape, some are more elongated than others, some are flat, and some are curled. Even the trunks of olive trees vary. Some grow quite straight, while others fan out more, and some, particularly as they age, grow thick and twisted with roots running atop the ground.

So which kind of olive tree am I to be? Could it be that God wants me to be the kind of olive tree he made me to be? Could it be that He doesn't want me to try and be some other kind of olive tree that He made someone else to be? I think the answer lies in a day of exploring all the beauty God gave us to behold . . . in Him, in His creation, and in ourselves.

Psalm 27:4 says, "I have asked one thing from the Lord; it is what I desire: to dwell in the house of the Lord all the days of my life, gazing on the beauty of the Lord and seeking him in his temple."

Read Psalm 19:1–6. How do you see God's beauty by looking around at what He has made?

In Hebrew, the word *glory* is *kavod*, and in Greek, *doxa*.[2] The glory of God can be defined as "brilliant, radiant beauty,"[3] the "weighty importance and shining majesty that accompany God's presence."[4] It can be described as the "manifest beauty of his holiness" or the "infinite beauty and greatness of his manifold perfections."[5]

Look up the following verses and write what they say about God's glory.

ISAIAH 6:3

PSALMS 72:19

If God's glory—His infinite beauty and shining majesty—fills the earth as Isaiah 6:3 and Psalm 72:19 describe, then can we see it? Feel it? Experience it? Record your thoughts.

We behold God's beauty by looking at—and meditating on—who He is.

We behold God's beauty by looking at—and meditating on—what He has made.

But there are other ways still.

When I first gave my life to Jesus fully, I could feel His transforming power begin to change me. I could feel His beauty begin to overtake the places in my life where I needed healing and wholeness. Scripture shows us that God's beauty is reflected in Jesus and His work on the cross.

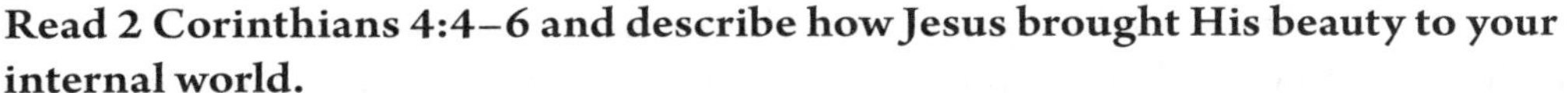

Read 2 Corinthians 4:4–6 and describe how Jesus brought His beauty to your internal world.

From the beginning, God made us in His image (Genesis 1:27). He made us to reflect His beauty. He made us to be olive trees who bloom for all to see and enjoy, but I'm not sure we consistently live as though this is all true. Understandably, we live in a world pressured and condemned to meet a standard of youthfulness and physical attractiveness as seen on magazine covers, in film and television, and on runways. Reality shows display this obsession weekly. Collectively as women, we spend billions annually trying to achieve the images created by media rather than the image created by God. Our society is obsessed with the public instead of the private. We've grown focused on age and aging instead of growing ageless, something I think God meant for us to do.

Have you really thought about what it means to be made in God's image? How does understanding that truth affect the way we process the world's pressure to meet its standard of beauty?

If we are made in God's image, and He is beautiful, then we are too. Every woman wants to be beautiful and feel beautiful. The good news is that God has called us beautiful from the beginning . . . of creation, of our lives, of when we became clothed in Christ (Galatians 3:27).

Read the following verses for clues about how God sees us as beautiful. Then use the chart to record how God created you to be beautiful versus how we often define beauty.

But the Lord said to Samuel, "Do not look at his appearance or his stature because I have rejected him. Humans do not see what the Lord sees, for humans see what is visible, but the Lord sees the heart."
1 SAMUEL 16:7

Those who look to him are radiant with joy; their faces will never be ashamed.
PSALM 34:5

Charm is deceptive and beauty is fleeting, but a woman who fears the Lord will be praised.
PROVERBS 31:30

"And why do you worry about clothes? Observe how the wildflowers of the field grow: They don't labor or spin thread. Yet I tell you that not even Solomon in all his splendor was adorned like one of these."
MATTHEW 6:28–29

"My Father is glorified by this: that you produce much fruit and prove to be my disciples."
JOHN 15:8

For we are his workmanship, created in Christ Jesus for good works, which God prepared ahead of time for us to do.
EPHESIANS 2:10

Don't let your beauty consist of outward things like elaborate hairstyles and wearing gold jewelry or fine clothes, but rather what is inside the heart—the imperishable quality of a gentle and quiet spirit, which is of great worth in God's sight.
1 PETER 3:3–4

HOW GOD CREATED ME TO BE BEAUTIFUL	HOW I OFTEN DEFINE BEAUTY

Oftentimes, our assessment of our own beauty is more about what we see in the mirror, and yet, we know from 1 Samuel 16:7 and 1 Peter 3:3–4, that God sees far more. He looks at our hearts. He looks at what is on the inside of us. He's called us to be olive trees. In fact, He says that our beauty will be like the olive tree. Of all the trees, this is the one He chose to describe Israel . . . to describe the church . . . and to describe us.[6]

His shoots will sprout,
And his beauty will be like the olive tree
And his fragrance like the cedars of Lebanon.
HOSEA 14:6 AMP

There is a beauty that comes with being a follower of Christ, isn't there? When you think of a beautiful Christian, what attributes come to mind?

PRAY

Leader (or volunteer) read the prayer aloud, or pray independently over your group before closing your time together.

God gave us beauty to behold. He made us beautiful to behold. Now, how do we take that beauty to our world?

Heavenly Father, show me how to take the beauty You gave me to behold and the beauty You placed inside of me to my world. Show me how to see like You see, to see others the way You see them. Help me to clothe myself the way You clothe me, with grace, goodness, holiness, righteousness, kindness, gentleness, tenderness, and love, that others will benefit. Help me to be like an olive tree, flourishing with blossoms, beautiful to behold. In Jesus' name, amen.

DAY 5 Guided Prayer and Journaling

> *But I am like a flourishing olive tree in the house of God;*
> *I trust in God's faithful love forever and ever.*
> PSALM 52:8

When I've walked through an olive tree farm in full bloom, or right before harvesting the olives, I've wanted to linger more than ever. I've wanted to take in the beauty, the fragrance, the breeze, the sunshine, the peace that seems to envelop me. In that moment, I want to stay as long as possible and soak in all I can.

When I linger with God, I feel much the same.

To *linger* is to stay in a place longer than necessary because of a reluctance to leave.[1]

Have you ever spent time with God to the point you were reluctant to leave?

Today, I want you to experience God's words differently than usual. I want you to posture yourself to hear from the Holy Spirit, to be less analytical, and settle yourself down to sit with Him. Let God's Word wash over you. Open yourself to what He might want you to feel, hear, see, and know.

We will do this every week on Day 5. We'll be making space to slow down and sit with the Holy Spirit. In John 14:26, Jesus told us that the Holy Spirit would teach us all things and remind us of all that Jesus said. I know for me it's better if I give myself time and space to stop and listen. To linger such that I'm reluctant to leave.

We are going to listen for God's leading and respond to what He wants to direct us to. I understand sitting and listening might be hard at first, particularly if you're not accustomed to sitting still at all. But it will be valuable and life-giving, I promise.

Psalm 46:10 says, "Be still, and know that I am God" (ESV). This is a practice that I want you to grow in until you feel reluctant to leave.

As we begin, let's start with this question: "God, what is one thing about the olive tree that You want me to take to heart?"

Next ask: "God, what is one verse You want to speak to me about from this week?" Write down that scripture here.

Now, I am going to encourage you to read aloud the verse you just wrote several times emphasizing a different word in that verse each time.

For example, when I do this with Psalm 52:8, here is what I do. I read it aloud several times with the emphasis on each word in sequence. For example:

- ***But*** *I am like a flourishing olive tree in the house of God . . .*
- *But* ***I*** *am like a flourishing olive tree in the house of God . . .*

Journal about where God is drawing your attention and any insight He gives you.

Finish your time by thanking God for His presence, His speaking, and all the ways He is at work in you to make you like a flourishing olive tree.

WEEK 2

Grafted into the Family

GROUP STUDY

Watch

Watch the video for Week 2: Grafted into the Family, recording your thoughts as you listen.

What if God's plan for us, especially for those who feel like outsiders, is like that of a master gardener?

To appreciate being "grafted in," we must first understand our natural separation.

By nature, we were the "wild branch"—separate from God's promises and without hope. This is not a statement of worthlessness, but of position.

Through Jesus, God performs the ultimate act of grafting, bringing us into His family not based on our merit, but on His grace.

You are not an afterthought or a second-class citizen in God's kingdom. You have been fully and completely accepted in the Beloved. (Ephesians 1:6)

The correct response to such a profound gift of grace is not pride, but deep humility.

> *You do not sustain the root, but the root sustains you.*
> ROMANS 11:18

Pride asks, "What have I done to deserve this?" Humility says, "I have done nothing to deserve this, and I am eternally grateful."

Discuss

Leader (or volunteer), read the following aloud to the group and follow with the prompts for discussion.

A number of years ago, our family went skiing in Colorado. Having grown up in Australia, I knew all about surfing, but not skiing. Still, on this vacation, I was determined to learn. The first day out, I had a great day skiing with the help of an instructor, and from my evaluation, I was confident I could go it alone the second day.

The next day when Nick joined me on the beginner slope, it was nothing short of perfect, until I made one serious mistake that led to another serious mistake. First, I asked Nick if he was glad that he did not go on the advanced slopes with the other guys and instead chose to stay and ski with me.

Being a man of integrity, he told me the truth. He said he would be having more fun with his friends, taking greater risks, and actually skiing more than snow-walking with me, but that he was still happy he had chosen to spend the day with me.

Well, I'll admit that was like putting a red rag in front of a bull. Shuffling forward on my skis, I looked back over my shoulder and utter some famous last words: "Eat my snow." About twenty seconds later, when I was mid-flight on my second unintentional somersault, I heard my knee go, "Pop, pop, pop," and I knew that I was in trouble. When I hit the ground with a thud and felt the most excruciating pain I'd ever known, I was sure of it. Nick rushed to my side and called for the ski patrol, who came and quickly loaded me into a rescue basket hooked to the back of snowmobile and towed me down the mountain to a waiting ambulance.

I later learned that I snapped my ACL, tore my MCL, tore my meniscus, and fractured my knee.

In case you're not familiar, the ACL is a ligament, and ligaments are tough bands of tissue that hold bones together. The ACL is located at the center of the knee joint. My injury required surgery to take a portion of my hamstring muscles and graft them in using strips of muscle to secure the torn ligament. The process of grafting restored my mobility. Without it I would have never been able to walk normally again.

It was in the months of my recovery that the scripture about us being grafted into the family of God came alive to me.

In the video, we saw that the imagery of the olive tree is the central metaphor that Paul used in Romans 11:17–24 to show us the masterful, merciful, and eternal plan of God to create a stunning, multi-ethnic family. Paul's metaphor about grafting is unique.

Instead of grafting a good branch onto a bad tree, God grafted a bad branch onto a good tree. "This was opposite of [how] first century people grafted olive trees. God had a good tree [of the Israelite nation] with a good root system [of the law]."[1] The Gentiles were the wild olive tree which God grafted into the good tree and its root system. Thus, the two plants fused and grafted together represent the Church.

When Paul wrote this metaphor, who was he speaking to?

What was he hoping to get across to the people? Fill in the blank.

An attitude of ____________________________

Understanding *who* Paul was writing to and *why* shows how the early Church could have been divided—and forgotten to be grateful.

Remember, grafting olive trees intends to take two kinds of plants and fuse them into one. Together, they can share the same rich roots, sun, rain, and seasons. Together, they can grow strong and bear fruit. Together, they can become something they can't be apart.

With this in mind, what does *being grafted into the family of God* mean to you?

Do you remember life before you were grafted into the family of God? Even if you can't remember a "before Jesus" season, we all can comprehend where we would be without Jesus. Write down specific ways that your life would be different, overall and daily, if Jesus had not rescued you.

Whatever our background and journey, none of us deserve our salvation (Ephesians 2:8).

Read Hebrews 2:1–4. Note how the writer describes being grafted into the family of God as so "great a salvation." How does your heart respond to your own salvation? Circle the words that describe your feelings.

Thankful	Grateful	Humbled	Awe
Reverent	Wonder	Included	Invited
Happy	Worshipful	Graced	Accepted

Are there other words you would use?

I remember realizing that Jesus died for me while I was yet a sinner; that He came for me in my brokenness and pain; and that He not only forgave me, but also gave me a new life, hope, and purpose on earth as part of a brand-new family. What kind of God would do that? Only Jesus.

GROW

Consider what you've seen and heard today and take action in your daily life applying this truth.

Journal about what your "great salvation" means to you. Reflect on what God has done in you, with you, for you, and through you. Then, worship Him over it all. Thank Him that He grafted you, a wild olive tree, into His family, into His cultivated tree, Jesus.

PRAY

Leader (or volunteer) read the prayer aloud, or pray independently over your group before closing your time together.

Heavenly Father, thank You for my so-great salvation. Thank You for how You have transformed me since I gave myself to You. I see what You've done, and no one else could have done all that for me. I open my heart and mind for You to continue healing me, transforming me, and growing me into being like the flourishing olive tree You've called me to be. In Jesus' name, amen.

WEEK 2 | Grafted into the Family

PERSONAL STUDY

The steady rhythm of daily devotion is a vital part of flourishing in your life with Jesus. Set aside time this week to really dig into God's Word. Each day, open yourself up to the Spirit's work in your heart and mind. Then, prayerfully reflect on the beautiful truth He is revealing during this season of new growth.

DAY 1 Accepted in the Beloved

Being Greek, being from an immigrant family, having olive-toned skin, and growing up in the poorest zip code in Sydney at the time, made me a target for ridicule and rejection more than anything else. I'll never forget the first time I heard our neighbor calling our family ethnic slurs. We had come home from attending our Greek Orthodox church and were headed into the house. I have no idea what prompted the verbal barrage. I was so young that I didn't fully understand, and yet, by the tone of her voice and by the reaction of my parents to get us kids in the house quickly, I instinctively understood more than I consciously realized.

Once I started school, I was called such derogatory names every day. I wasn't ever sure why, but I knew that being Greek was a reason I was not accepted by the other kids.

When I learned to read, I discovered that all the graffiti I passed everyday walking to school was directed at me and every person of different ethnicities living in our community. As if it wasn't enough having to listen to being called names, now I got to read them.

Though I learned to be a tough girl and excel in academics and sports, I'm not sure I ever quit being "different." In elementary school, Mum would drop me off at ballet, and as soon as she was out of sight, I'd drop my tutu and run across the street to play soccer with the boys. When she'd take me shopping and lead me to the dolls in the toy department, I'd wander over to the books. Though I always knew Mum loved me deeply, I couldn't help but think she didn't know what to do with me. She'd adopted a little girl and probably had all these dreams of little girly things, and here I was a bit more rough and tumble with an unquenchable thirst for knowledge.

I have two girls, and I want them to experience what I didn't growing up—acceptance. I want them both to know that they are fully loved exactly as God made them to be. God put gifts and talents in them for His glory and their flourishing. I do not want to quench or thwart the purposes of God in their lives by not accepting the fact that they are different from me.

I feel certain that we all have our stories of not being accepted, because of our ethnicity, our gender, our socioeconomic status, our education, or our professional position. Because we weren't enough of something—athletic enough, pretty enough, tall enough, fit enough, wealthy enough, connected enough, and on the list could go. There will always be reasons some people don't accept us, but the good news is that God always accepts us.

Still, we're often left with the task of sorting through all the emotions that come with being rejected, or at least trying to. We know the feeling of being blindsided by it, the shame that overcomes us, the confusion that floods our minds, the guilt and condemnation that send us spinning, ruminating on every word we said, and they said . . . and all we didn't get to say. I've had my fair share of these emotions and the sleepless nights that go along with them, as I imagine you have too. And while I don't want us to relive too many painful memories, to start, I do want us to unpack what it means to be rejected and not accepted for who we are and as we are.

Using the chart that follows, I want us to walk through a four-step exercise.

In the first row, list some significant times when you felt rejected, the kind of rejection that stuck with you.

In the second row, write what you began to believe about yourself. Rejection can be so painful that we think untrue things about ourselves. Because of the rejection I faced early in life, I grew up believing I was unworthy, unlovable, and deeply flawed.

In the third row, if you feel you've been healed or have overcome a particular time of rejection, describe what it took for you to live free.

In the fourth row, if you renewed your mind with a scripture to overcome an instance of rejection, include it.

WHEN I WAS REJECTED	
WHAT IT TRIED TO MAKE ME BELIEVE ABOUT MYSELF	
HOW I WAS HEALED AND OVERCAME	
BIBLE VERSES THAT GOT ME THROUGH	

I'm not sure any of us would disagree that one of the most common battles of our generation is seeking acceptance on social media. One study regarding adolescents has reported that those "who use social media for more than three hours per day are at an increased risk for developing mental health problems. They are specifically at risk for mental health issues, including anxiety, depression, suicidal thoughts, negative self-image, and loneliness."[1] I would venture to say this is not a problem limited to our youth.

How much time do you spend on social media each day, especially counting likes, scrolling through comments, and comparing your life to someone else's?

I know that last question might have felt quite painful. I think it's an "ouch" for most of us, especially with our phones and social media accounts so accessible.

At the same time, I'm well aware that the last thing any of us want to feel is rejected, and we're desperate to know if our friends saw our post, if they liked it, if they commented words of affirmation. But the fact remains, not everyone will see our post and like it. On social media and in real life, we will be rejected, not once, not twice, but most likely on the daily.

Rejection is so painful and can rob us of our peace, joy, and confidence. I want you to know that everyone experiences rejection because not everyone everywhere will always like you, approve of you, or accept you . . . or me. The truth is that even Jesus experienced rejection at the hands of people.

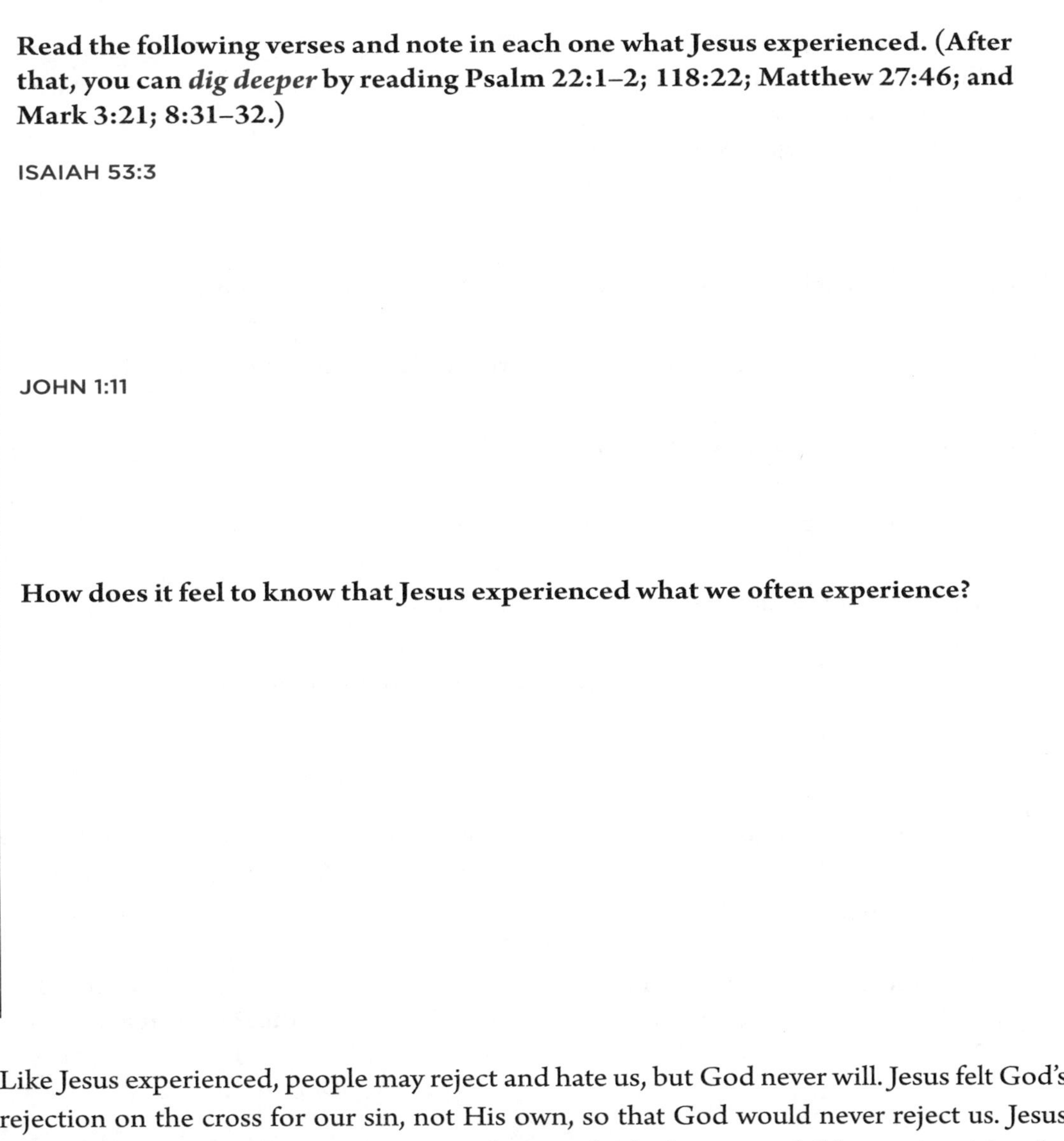

Read the following verses and note in each one what Jesus experienced. (After that, you can *dig deeper* by reading Psalm 22:1–2; 118:22; Matthew 27:46; and Mark 3:21; 8:31–32.)

ISAIAH 53:3

JOHN 1:11

How does it feel to know that Jesus experienced what we often experience?

Like Jesus experienced, people may reject and hate us, but God never will. Jesus felt God's rejection on the cross for our sin, not His own, so that God would never reject us. Jesus demonstrated this. When society rejected or overlooked women, children, minorities, the sick, the oppressed, and the poor, Jesus saw them and loved them. He healed them, saved them, and included them.

Consider the following verses regarding:
1) Who Jesus accepted,
2) What He did to accept them, and
3) Why they were rejected by society.[2]

He spoke to women (John 4:27).

He accepted financial support from women for His ministry (Luke 8:1–3).

He made His first appearance after His resurrection to women (Luke 24:1–11).

He healed the unclean (Mark 1:40–45; Luke 8:48).

He recognized the poor and the oppressed (Luke 4:18; 6:20; 14:13–14).

He loved across racial divides (Luke 10:25–37; John 4:4–42).

He promised never to reject anyone who comes to Him (John 6:37).

Jesus promised each one of us something precious, and John recorded it: "All that My Father gives Me will come to Me; and the one who comes to Me I will most certainly not cast out" (John 6:37 AMP). In other words, *I will never, never reject anyone who follows Me.*

Take a moment to reflect on what this truly means to you. Do you feel accepted by God? Or do you feel you have to perform for His acceptance? Or is it a little of both?

There is power in knowing God accepts us. Consider the following verses and personalize them to strengthen your faith in knowing you are accepted in the Beloved.

You are seen.

> *I will instruct you and show you the way to go; with my eye on you, I will give counsel.*
> PSALM 32:8

You are known.

> *For it was you who created my inward parts; you knit me together in my mother's womb. I will praise you because I have been remarkably and wondrously made. Your works are wondrous, and I know this very well.*
> PSALM 139:13–14

You are loved.

> *Who can separate us from the love of Christ? Can affliction or distress or persecution or famine or nakedness or danger or sword? . . . For I am persuaded that neither death nor life, nor angels nor rulers, nor things present nor things to come, nor powers, nor height nor depth, nor any other created thing will be able to separate us from the love of God that is in Christ Jesus our Lord.*
> ROMANS 8:35, 38–39

You are chosen.

> *For he chose us in him, before the foundation of the world, to be holy and blameless in love before him.*
> EPHESIANS 1:4

You are accepted . . . in the Beloved . . . therefore accept one another.

> *Therefore, accept each other just as Christ has accepted you so that God will be given glory.*
> ROMANS 15:7 NLT

Good job today! We went to some hard places and did some serious soul searching. I know you want to be like a flourishing olive tree in the house of God. I hope that in the hard you will find more healing and wholeness in Jesus this week. I hope you feel more accepted in the Beloved than you ever have.

PRAY

Leader (or volunteer) read the prayer aloud, or pray independently over your group before closing your time together.

As we close out our day, my prayer for you is based on the passage we examined earlier, Ephesians 1:3–6.

Bless the God and Father of our Lord Jesus Christ, who has blessed us with every spiritual blessing in the heavenly places in Christ . . . we are eternally grateful that You chose us before the foundation of the world, that we should be holy and without blame before You, having predestined us to adoption as daughters by Jesus Christ to Himself, according to the good pleasure of His will, to the praise of the glory of His grace, by which He made us ACCEPTED IN THE BELOVED.

DAY 2 The Grace of God

Welcome back—I'm so proud of you! Together, we are like flourishing olive trees in the house of God. Today, roll up your sleeves because we're going to dig deep into my favorite word—*grace*.

Most of us know the song *Amazing Grace*, but do we really know how amazing grace is? Grace is mentioned roughly one hundred seventy times in the Bible.[1] It's a word Paul used as a greeting in each of his letters: "Grace and peace unto you," he said thirteen times.[2] If you start digging, you might find grace inexhaustible. We've been saved by grace (Ephesians 2:8–9); we have been given grace upon grace (John 1:16–17); we are under grace (Romans 6:14); we are to grow in grace (2 Peter 3:18); we are to be strong in grace (2 Timothy 2:1); we are empowered by grace (Titus 2:11–12); we can fall from grace (Galatians 5:4); we can be restored by God's grace (1 Peter 5:10); we are to go to the throne of grace (Hebrews 4:16); grace is sufficient (2 Corinthians 12:9); grace is something to set our hope on (1 Peter 1:13); grace was given to us before the beginning of time (2 Timothy 1:9); grace is something we can speak (Colossians 4:6); and Jesus was anointed with grace (Psalm 45:2). Whew! That's just scratching the surface, and today, I want you to be overwhelmed again by grace.

SAVING GRACE

God's grace is defined as His "unmerited favor."[3] The Bible tells us grace is what saves us by faith; that grace is a gift God freely gives us. In the words of one commentary, "the grace that saves is the free, undeserved goodness and favour of God; and he saves, not by the works of the law, but through faith in Christ Jesus."[4]

I want you to see this for yourself in the Word. Ephesians 2:8–9 says, "For you are saved by grace through faith, and this is not from yourselves; it is God's gift—not from works, so that no one can boast."

Romans 3:10–12 explains why we can't earn the gift of grace: "There is no one righteous, not even one. There is no one who understands; there is no one who seeks God. All have turned away; all alike have become worthless. There is no one who does what is good, not even one."

You can respond to God's grace in two ways. You can be offended (the self-righteous way) or you can be in awe (the humble way).

In Luke 18:9–14, Jesus told a parable that reflects these two different ways to respond to God's grace. Write down differences in the behavior and the words of the two men in the parable.

	PHARISEE (SELF-RIGHTEOUS)	TAX COLLECTOR (HUMBLE)
DID		
SAID		

When you first experienced God's grace and gave your life to Jesus fully, were you in awe? Did you respond like the tax collector? Write a few sentences to thank God for His grace.

SANCTIFYING GRACE

Encountering grace when we first give our lives to Jesus only begins our experience of grace. We receive more as we know both what grace is and what grace does.

Consider Peter's experience of grace. Record what you feel after reading the passage below. Moreover, imagine yourself in his shoes and what it must have felt like for him spiritually and emotionally. (To *dig deeper* you can also read Luke 22:31–34.)

JOHN 21:1–19

We need to receive God's grace again and again, day after day. Of course, we don't deserve it any more than Peter did. But God gives us grace because grace makes us more like Him.

Read Titus 2:11–13 and list three things that grace does for us.

1.

2.

3.

How has the grace of God helped you in one of these ways?

SUFFICIENT GRACE

Paul endured much suffering. He was flogged five times with thirty-nine lashes, beaten with rods, pelted with stones, shipwrecked, rejected, hungry, and more (2 Corinthians 11:23–27). He must have also experienced great emotional suffering, being betrayed and harmed by many during his ministry. He was even given a thorn in the flesh, a messenger of Satan to torment him . . . and yet, God's great grace sustained him through it all (2 Corinthians 12:7).

Sufficient grace means that God's grace is enough for us to stand, no matter what challenge we are facing, whether from within ourselves or from the world around us. Sometimes we need grace to overcome the battle within first. Early in my walk with Jesus, my own shame, guilt, and perfectionism made it difficult to believe God loved me and forgave me. It took years to receive His grace fully. Other times we need His grace to overcome the battle from without—to stand through physical, circumstantial, or spiritual hardship. Every minute of the day, we need God's grace in our parenting, marriage, job, ministry, leadership, health, education, temperament, perspective, and decision-making.

Let's explore further what it means for God's grace to be sufficient in our lives. In the verse below, circle the four things the "God of all grace" will do for you.

> *The God of all grace, who called you to his eternal glory in Christ, will himself restore, establish, strengthen, and support you after you have suffered a little while.*
> 1 PETER 5:10

Did you notice the phrase at the end of the verse? It says ". . . after you have suffered a little while." This can be translated as "to a small extent."[5] The God of all grace promises to restore, establish, strengthen, and support us after we've suffered to a small extent. God does not minimize our sufferings, but they will not even be a blink of an eye in eternity. What a promise!

SERVING GRACE

After saving grace, sanctifying grace, and sufficient grace, there is serving grace. In 2 Corinthians 9:8, Paul assures that "God is able to make every grace overflow to you, so that in every way, always having everything you need, you may excel in every good work."

We are saved by grace, not by works, but we are saved by grace for good works. Works can't save us. Only grace does. Grace then helps us do good works.

> **Look up Ephesians 2:10 and write it here.**

When we're competent in something, we easily become self-sufficient and independent. God wants us to be proficient, while we remain dependent on His grace.

SURPASSING GRACE

After all we've seen about grace so far, we have to get understanding about one more thing before we wrap up: We can grow in grace, and we are to maintain grace.

> **Look up 2 Peter 3:18. Write what it says and underline the first sentence.**

> **We're to grow in God's extravagant grace, but how? The early Christians grew in grace by devoting themselves to four things. Look up Acts 2:42 and list them here.**
>
> 1.
>
> 2.
>
> 3.
>
> 4.

How can you incorporate these practices into your modern life?

We dug deep today! Good job! There's so much more to grace than we covered, but I hope you are beginning to see how *amazing* grace is. I hope to persuade you to *continue* in the grace of God! (Acts 13:43).

PRAY

Leader (or volunteer) read the prayer aloud, or pray independently over your group before closing your time together.

As we close out our day, my prayer for you is based on 2 Timothy 1:9 and Hebrews 4:16.

Heavenly Father, You have called each and every one of us, according to Your grace, to fulfill Your plans and purposes for our lives. You've saved us with Your grace, called us with Your grace, filled us with Your grace, empowered us with Your grace, and we want to continue in Your grace—Your grace that is sufficient for everything we will face today. So, we come boldly to the throne of grace and ask You to please give us the grace we need to continue fulfilling all that You've called us to do. In Jesus' name, amen.

DAY 3 Humbled

When I turned fifty, I decided that I wanted to keep learning and growing, so I started a Masters in Evangelism and Leadership at Wheaton College. I prefer to do things in community, so I decided to launch Propel Cohorts in partnership with Wheaton so I could study with and learn from other women. It was one of the best experiences of my life, and four years later, I graduated with the first cohort to complete the program. I am committed to being a lifelong learner, so I can continue to be fruitful in doing what I'm called to do.

I wish I could tell you it was easy from the start, but it was far from it. I remember the first day I showed up for class for my masters; I felt so out of place. Most of my classmates were in their twenties and thirties and not too many years since they'd last been in school. But for me, it had been decades since I'd been in a classroom. When I attended my last college course, the professor sat next to an overhead projector and wrote on the plastic surface of it with colored markers. My classmates and I stared up at the projection screen hanging against the wall reading all that the professor wrote. Then we took notes in a spiral notebook using a ballpoint pen. Antiquated I know, but that was the best thing back then. Now the professor walks around with a clicker in his hand as pages of information appear on a smart board, and I type notes on a laptop.

When they passed out the syllabus and went over all that we needed to know for turning in assignments, I felt overwhelmed. I couldn't get over how much there was to learn before I could start learning what I had come to school to learn. In other words, there was software to master, portals with passwords to understand, and virtual libraries to navigate. For a woman with a BA in English who loves books, it was hard to comprehend that I couldn't physically walk to the campus library and leave with a stack of books. When Catherine or Sophia would see me watching a YouTube video to learn how to use another kind of software, they would quickly offer to help. "There's a much easier way to do that," they'd often say. They had grown up attending school with the latest technology. Their phones were loaded with all the apps and all the shortcuts that schools often use today. As humiliating as it sometimes was, I was well aware that if I wanted to keep growing and moving forward, I needed to learn from them. So I did. With their help, I built an entirely new set of skills.

I choose to be willing to grow, stretch, become a novice, and potentially fail. I know from experience that the moment we think we've arrived, we will move out of humility and into a place we don't want to be.

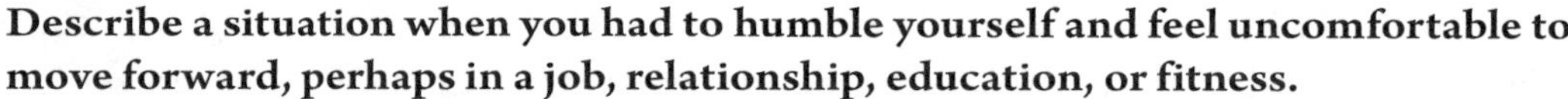

Describe a situation when you had to humble yourself and feel uncomfortable to move forward, perhaps in a job, relationship, education, or fitness.

Humility is essential for us who are grafted in, saved by grace, and who can do nothing apart from Jesus (John 15:5). Humility is "the personal quality of being free from arrogance and pride and having an accurate estimate of one's worth."[1] It's the opposite of entitlement, "the belief that one is inherently deserving of privileges or special treatment."[2]

List some synonyms or descriptive ideas of what it means to be humble.

What comes to my mind about humility is being teachable, approachable, authentic, grateful, forgiving, gracious, and reliant on faith in Jesus. Did any of those make your list?

Let's keep going so we discover what the Bible says about being humble.

In the Old Testament, only one man was ever called humble . . . and it was God who said he was. Numbers 12:3 tells us, "Moses was a very humble man, more so than anyone on the face of the earth."

While I fully trust that Moses wrote what God said, isn't it a little humorous that Moses wrote this about himself? God had done the miraculous through Moses in many situations. It was Moses who led the Israelites out of captivity in Egypt, parted the Red Sea, carried the actual tablets of the Ten Commandments, and saw the back of God when he asked to see His glory. Yet Moses was called more humble than anyone on the face of the earth!

This shows that when we get up close and personal with God, we truly understand that God is God and we are not. Therein lies the key to understanding true humility.

Sometimes, though, we confuse humility with low self-esteem or thinking less of oneself.

A popular quote helps clarify the difference, "Humility is not thinking less of yourself; but thinking of yourself less."[3] Humility is about having a right view of ourselves in relationship to him. It's about knowing who we are in Him—and that we are a wild olive tree who has been grafted into the family of God!

The ultimate example of humility is Jesus. Paul exhorts us to have the same attitude as Jesus—an attitude of humility. Read Philippians 2:3–11 and list how Paul describes humility. I found at least five things, but you might find more.

1.

2.

3.

4.

5.

Draw a star by the ones you struggle with personally.

Jesus emptied Himself, took on the form of a servant, humbled Himself, and then God exalted Him. Did you notice that?

God's Word shows this pattern. Read either James 4:10 or 1 Peter 5:6 and write what you find.

Clearly, we have both the ability and the responsibility to humble ourselves consistently. If we don't, Jesus gave us a sobering reminder of what will happen. Look up either Matthew 23:12 or Luke 14:11, and write what that reminder is.

We have a responsibility to keep humbling ourselves. Why do you think that is?

We have to keep humbling ourselves because we're in danger of forgetting who exalted us and why. If God chooses to exalt us, it will always be for His glory, not ours. God says that the way up is down, so we don't have to try to hustle, platform, promote, and influence. We simply need to humble ourselves. Our hearts are always prone to think higher of ourselves than we ought—and that's a sure pathway to destruction.

While humility looks up to God, pride looks side to side. Pride always leads to mistreating people. It produces a vibe that says, *I am better than you; I am more holy than you; I am more worthy than you*; or *I am more deserving than you*. If we are not careful, feelings of superiority and self-righteousness can creep into our hearts, and there is nothing more unbiblical than thinking we are better than someone else. Yet, because of our humanity, I imagine that we've all done it at one time or another.

When have pride and feelings of superiority and entitlement begun to creep into your life? And what have been the consequences?

In the video teaching for this week, I mentioned some verses about pride. Read the one that follows. (After that, you can *dig deeper* and read Proverbs 11:2; 16:5, 18; Jeremiah 9:23; and James 4:6.)

To fear the LORD is to hate evil. I hate arrogant pride, evil conduct, and perverse speech.
PROVERBS 8:13

Jesus demonstrated a posture of humility. The word *posture* reminds me of my Mum. "Christina," she would say, "Mind your posture. Sit up." I would get frustrated because I preferred to slouch. It was easy and more comfortable. Now, like Mum, I remind my own girls of their posture, physically *and* spiritually. A Greek word for humble is *tapeinóō*, which can mean "lowly in spirit."[4] Some translations describe Jesus as "lowly in spirit." That was His posture, and how we're to walk spiritually.

Colossians 3:12 tells us we're to clothe ourselves in humility. We're to "put [it] on" just like we would a piece of clothing. Perhaps by wrapping ourselves in it, we won't lose the feeling of being ever so grateful for all that God has done for us and how far He's brought us.

When we lose sight of all God has done for us, it's so easy to stop being humble, isn't it? That's when our posture begins to slouch and we stop being lowly in spirit, and spiritual pride begins to creep in.

If you want to *dig deeper*, read the following verses that speak to our spiritual posture, and write down what you find: Micah 6:8; John 3:30; 12:24–25; Romans 12:3, 16; and Ephesians 4:1–3.

Consciously look for an opportunity to humble yourself today. You'll know the opportunity because it will feel uncomfortable. I know because that's how it often feels to me. Capture that feeling and turn it into a practice. Challenge yourself to walk in a posture of humility, always, just like Jesus modeled for us.

PRAY

Leader (or volunteer) read the prayer aloud, or pray independently over your group before closing your time together.

Heavenly Father, I humble myself before You, that You may exalt me at the proper time. I choose a humble posture, one that is willing to learn, stays curious about others, wants the best for others, listens well, and cares deeply. Help me to believe what You say over anyone else's opinion, including my own. Help me to trust in Your protection rather than spend my energy protecting myself. Help me to remember that my identity is in You, that You have my back, and I am free to elevate everyone around me. I am so grateful for the life You have given me—a life in You. In Jesus' name, amen.

DAY 4 Invited

"Mummy," Sophia quietly began, fidgeting with the covers on her bed, "Angela invited the girls to her house . . . but not me." Sophia was in middle school, and she had been excluded by her besties. "She's been talking about me and making fun of me," Sophia said, lips trembling. Laying with her while we talked and prayed was one of my favorite times of the day. Our expressive girl who loved to sing and act had been more withdrawn recently, so I knew something was up. I'd gently prodded and prayed, and now it was finally spilling out all over the place. "I saw them all pointing and talking about me at play practice," she continued.

Her tender heart was utterly broken, and the more she talked, the more mine was too. I cried with her, hearing the confusion and pain, and imagining her sweet, freckled face reddened with shame. As I held Sophia to comfort and soothe her, I was actually consoling us both. I had been through this with Catherine just a few years earlier, and I was well aware that some things about middle school never change.[1] One day you're *in* with the friend group, and the next day you find yourself on the outside looking in, wondering why you're *out* and not getting invited to the most recent party.

Think back to when you were in school—when you and your friends decided who was *in* and who was *out*. What were the criteria for being *in* or *out*?

YOU WERE IN IF YOU WERE . . .	YOU WERE OUT IF YOU WERE . . .

Look at your list. Circle all the words that would have described your ten-, eleven-, or twelve-year-old self.

I'm glad that we're not in middle school anymore, and I hope we've grown in how we relate to others. That said, the underlying reason why we categorize people remains the same as it did then. Prejudice. A *prejudice* is "an adverse opinion or leaning formed without just grounds or before sufficient knowledge."[2] It's a bias—a "preconceived judgment."[3]

What subtle prejudices creep into our lives and influence who we consider *in* and *out* at work, school, church, or where we volunteer? Write down any that come to mind.

Jesus often acknowledged, healed, and respected someone who was *out* in front of people who were *in*. Read the following stories and pick out the characters who were *in* and *out*. (You can also *dig deeper* by looking at Matthew 9:27–34; 15:21–31; Luke 8:26–39, 43–48; and John 4:1–42.)

	PERSON JESUS MINISTERED TO WHO WAS "OUT"	ONLOOKERS WHO WERE CONSIDERED "IN"
MATTHEW 9:9–13 *The Call of Matthew*		
MARK 10:13–16 *The Children*		
LUKE 7:36–50 *The Woman Who Anointed His Feet*		
JOHN 5:1–16 *The Man at the Pool*		

Can you identify the prejudices in these stories? Describe them here.

Everyone Jesus ministered to in these stories, He invited. He included. He extended His grace.

- To Matthew the tax collector, He said, "Follow me."
- To the children, "Let the little children come to me."
- To the woman who anointed His feet with perfume, "Your sins are forgiven."
- To the lame man at the pool of Bethesda, He said, "Get up! Pick up your mat and walk."

Can you think of any other people in the Gospels that Jesus invited? Who do you think He is inviting today?

Before Jesus left this earth, He commissioned us to continue what He began—to keep inviting people. Matthew 28:19–20 records Jesus saying, "Go, therefore, and make disciples of all nations, baptizing them in the name of the Father and of the Son and of the Holy Spirit, teaching them to observe everything I have commanded you."

How might we deal with our own hearts and invite people we don't particularly like, perhaps because they are different from us?

I imagine when we get to the Marriage Supper of the Lamb—where the Church will be united with Jesus—we will find a number of people we never expected to be there, perhaps because they didn't vote, dress, look, or eat like us. I'm glad that Jesus invites *everyone*.

Look up Romans 10:11–13 and 1 Timothy 2:1–4 in the CSB and fill in the blanks.

For the Scripture says, ______________________________ who believes on him will not be put to shame, since there is no distinction between Jew and Greek, because the same Lord of all richly blesses all who call on him. For ________________________ who calls on the name of the Lord will be saved.

ROMANS 10:11–13

First of all, then, I urge that petitions, prayers, intercessions, and thanksgivings be made for everyone, for kings and all those who are in authority, so that we may lead a tranquil and quiet life in all godliness and dignity. This is good, and it pleases God our Savior, who wants ____ to be saved and to come to the knowledge of the truth.

1 TIMOTHY 2:1–4

Everyone literally means "every person"[4]—regardless of class, gender, ethnicity, race, culture, past, beliefs, age, occupation, community, status, and every other way our society can be sorted.

In your world, who would you identify as *everyone*?

Who is God highlighting to you today? Who does He want you to invite to meet Him? Is it the person who styles your hair, repairs your car, manicures your nails, or works out next to you at the gym? Perhaps the co-worker in the cubicle or office next to you? Or the parent you bump into at every one of your child's games? Is it someone you've often thought of as *in* or *out*?

Write the person's name here that God highlighted to you and think about them for a moment.

PRAY

Leader (or volunteer) read the prayer aloud, or pray independently over your group before closing your time together.

As we end our day together, let's pray for the person God highlighted to you. Let's pray according to 1 Timothy 2:1–4 that we read earlier by inviting the Holy Spirit to till the soil of our hearts and theirs to be receptive to His will that *everyone* be saved.

Heavenly Father, thank You for highlighting ______________________________ to me. I want them to come to know You. Holy Spirit, please lead me and show me how to befriend them more, how to be salt and light in the places where they are walking in darkness. Help me to love them unconditionally with Your love and see them without any prejudice. I pray for their salvation, that they would receive Your invitation to be grafted into the kingdom of Your family. In Jesus' name, amen.

DAY 5 Guided Prayer and Journaling

> *But I am like a flourishing olive tree in the house of God;*
> *I trust in God's faithful love forever and ever.*
> PSALM 52:8

Let's finish our week strong. Let's seek to be led and transformed by the Spirit of God as we meditate on the Word of God.

Go back through this week's study and ask God to draw your attention to a verse for reflection. Write it here.

As we look at that verse, remember the goal of Day 5 of our study. It's not only for us to get into the Word of God, but also to get the Word of God into us. It's for us to be led by the Spirit of God—as a child of God—to cooperate with all the transformation He wants to do in us through His Word. Psalm 16:11 sets the tone perfectly for our time with God today: "You make known to me the path of life; in your presence there is fullness of joy; at your right hand are pleasures forevermore" (ESV).

In Your presence . . .

That's where we want to be—in God's presence.

What is the best way for you to get into His presence?

It can be different for us all.

Perhaps you should put your phone away for a while or sing worship songs, fixing your eyes upon Him as He stills your soul. Maybe you should take a walk in nature with the verse above in mind.

As you seek His presence, pray, "God, I believe You are drawing my attention to this verse. Would You, by Your Spirit, direct me and help me to discern the work You are wanting to do in me today?

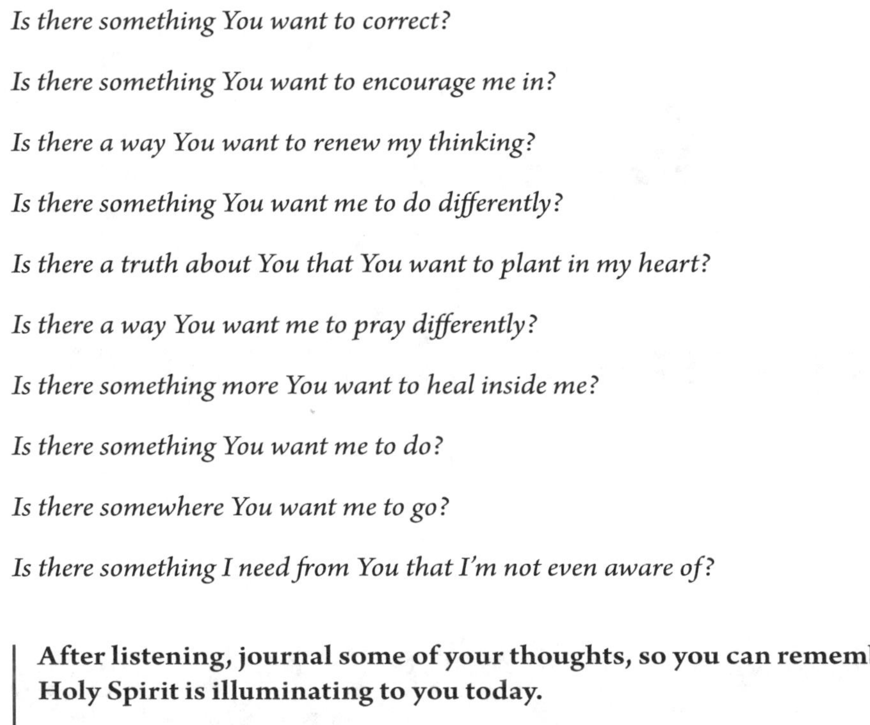

Is there something You want to correct?

Is there something You want to encourage me in?

Is there a way You want to renew my thinking?

Is there something You want me to do differently?

Is there a truth about You that You want to plant in my heart?

Is there a way You want me to pray differently?

Is there something more You want to heal inside me?

Is there something You want me to do?

Is there somewhere You want me to go?

Is there something I need from You that I'm not even aware of?

After listening, journal some of your thoughts, so you can remember what the Holy Spirit is illuminating to you today.

Finally, thank God for His presence, His speaking, and all the ways He is making you like a flourishing olive tree in His house, trusting in Him forever and ever.

WEEK 3

Branches of Peace

GROUP STUDY

Watch

Watch the video for Week 3: Branches of Peace, recording your thoughts as you listen.

We all desire peace, but what does true, lasting peace look like, and how do we obtain it in a world filled with conflict and anxiety?

The first mention of an olive branch in the Bible is a powerful testament to God's faithfulness and His memory of His promises.

> *Then God remembered Noah.*
> GENESIS 8:1 NKJV

The olive branch was physical proof that God had not forgotten His people. It was a sign of new beginnings and hope.

The story of Noah assures us that God always remembers His promises and acts on them in His perfect time.

> ***Shalom*** (Hebrew): More than tranquility, it signifies wholeness, completeness, well-being, and a right relationship with God.
>
> ***Eiréné*** (Greek): This is the peace that comes from reconciliation with God through Christ.

As recipients of God's peace, we are called to be conduits of that peace to others.

> *"Blessed are the peacemakers, for they will be called children of God."*
> MATTHEW 5:9 NIV

Discuss

Leader (or volunteer), read the following aloud to the group and follow with the prompts for discussion.

Genesis 8 opens with three beautiful words full of mercy and grace: "God remembered Noah."

God has never forgotten nor can He forget anyone or anything. God knows everything immediately, comprehensively, perfectly, and eternally. God did not lose track of Noah and His family. Instead, He remembered them in the sense that He was about to act on the promise He made to establish His covenant with Noah (Genesis 6:18).

We've just learned of the olive branch as a universal symbol of peace. The first biblical appearance of an olive leaf, in Genesis 8:11, served as a sign of hope and fulfilled promise to Noah.

When the dove came to him at evening, there was a plucked olive leaf in its beak. So Noah knew that the water on the earth's surface had gone down (Genesis 8:11).

Reflect on a time you were waiting for a "sign of life" from God during a difficult season. What did it feel like when that sign of hope appeared?

How does knowing that "God remembered Noah" before the olive leaf appeared reinforce your trust in His faithfulness, even when you cannot yet see evidence of His promises?

There is a clear distinction between the world's version of peace (a temporary absence of conflict) and biblical peace.

Do you remember from the video what a whole perspective is? Explain it in your own words.

A whole perspective takes into account someone's weaknesses as well as their strengths, both the things they've gotten wrong and the things they've gotten right. God didn't just remember Noah's shortcomings and sin; God remembered Noah's righteousness as well. Because God is a peacemaker, He brought peace with a whole perspective. As His image-bearers, we are to do the same, and we need a whole perspective to do it.

We are challenged to move beyond being "peacekeepers" (who often avoid conflict) to becoming active "peacemakers" (who work toward reconciliation), as encouraged in Matthew 5:9.

Describe a situation where you chose to keep the peace to avoid a difficult conversation. Looking back, what might it have looked like to be a peacemaker instead?

Being a peacemaker requires "speaking the truth in love" (Ephesians 4:15). Why are both truth and love essential components for genuine reconciliation?

Extending an olive branch is a tangible act of peacemaking. It is often the first step toward mending a broken relationship, and it requires significant humility and courage.

Without sharing specific details that would betray confidence, think of a relationship in your life that needs reconciliation. What is the biggest obstacle preventing you from extending an olive branch?

Read aloud together: "If possible, as far as it depends on you, live at peace with everyone" (Romans 12:18).

What does the phrase "as far as it depends on you" mean for your responsibility in pursuing peace, especially when the other person may not be receptive?

The ultimate source of our peace is Christ Himself, the Prince of Peace.

How can we as a group be a source of encouragement and accountability for one another as we seek to both receive God's peace and extend it to others this week?

How can we specifically pray for one another in this area?

GROW

Consider what you've seen and heard today and take action in your daily life applying this truth.

Peace has an intention to extend hope.

Take the peace that comes from Christ within you into your day.

If you step into a situation with tension, be a peacemaker—something we'll learn more about this week in your homework.

Extend all the hope you can where you can.

PRAY

Leader (or volunteer) read the prayer aloud, or pray independently over your group before closing your time together.

Heavenly Father, I'm so grateful that You have made me to be a peacemaker, someone who can extend an olive branch graciously. Help me to walk in peace and take it into relationships and situations everywhere I can. Help me to bring hope into what feels hopeless. In Jesus' name, amen.

WEEK 3 | Branches of Peace

PERSONAL STUDY

The steady rhythm of daily devotion is a vital part of flourishing in your life with Jesus. Set aside time this week to really dig into God's Word. Each day, open yourself up to the Spirit's work in your heart and mind. Then, prayerfully reflect on the beautiful truth He is revealing during this season of new growth.

DAY 1
The Prince of Peace

DAY 2
Finding Inner Peace

DAY 3
Blessed Are the Peacemakers

DAY 4
Flip Some Tables

DAY 5
Guided Prayer and Journaling

DAY 1 The Prince of Peace

When Sophia was wrapping up her high school years, like most seniors, it was time to get serious about picking colleges and selecting a major. For months she stressed over her grades, picking the right school, applying for scholarships, writing essays for her college applications, and sweating whether she'd get into her favorite school or not. Then there was the question of whether she needed to attend college at all, as she was mostly interested in doing stand-up comedy. She's always been hilariously funny, but Nick and I had no experience in how to coach her when it came to pursuing such a career. When she wondered all this aloud, she was also concerned about getting to go to the same school as one of her friends or having to make all new friends. And with all the wars and chaos happening around the globe, there were times she voiced concerns about whether there would even be a world in which to find a job when she graduated. I imagine most students have such thoughts from time to time, perhaps even questioning if God cares about this world at all. I assure you He does.

I think we'd all agree that we all have the capacity to go *there* don't we? Like Sophia did, going there is where our minds spin with worrying thoughts. I call this the "what if" road, and I'm sure you've traveled it in your journey.

What if things don't go as planned? *What if* I lose my job? *What if* there really is something seriously wrong with my body? *What if* I never marry? *What if* I don't get accepted into the program? *What if* we break up or divorce? *What if* the market keeps falling? *What if* . . . ?

On this road, we often feel helpless to stop the unraveling, and in seconds we go from peace to panic, from wonder to worry, from trusting to terrified. Our palms can sweat, a knot can grow in our stomachs, a fog can cloud our minds, and a twitching or tightness can fill our bodies.

We tend to think that we are trusting in God and that trusting is easy *until* . . . we start to lose control of the things we've worked so hard to control—such as our children, marriages, homes, schedules, friendships, education, careers, savings, or spiritual lives. When we face a bigger or different crisis, we realize we have more room to grow and mature. More room to trust. We need peace once more, and it's the kind of peace only God can give.

The Hebrew word for peace is *shalom*, which "relates to a relationship of love and loyalty with God and one another." It means "welfare, prosperity, or wholeness as well as the absence of hostility . . . the antithesis of harm . . . and [it is used] as a synonym for what is good."[1]

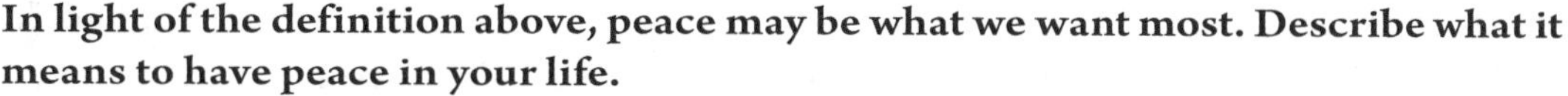

In light of the definition above, peace may be what we want most. Describe what it means to have peace in your life.

There are times in all our lives when we feel desperate for peace—in our thoughts, in our hearts, in our physical bodies—and as much as we might go in search of it in places other than God, we don't often find it there. And even if we do, it's not true peace. Sure, we may find a temporary release or fix or escape, but I think we'd all agree none of that is lasting peace. When we numb ourselves binge-watching a series or scrolling through our phones or over-eating, drinking, or medicating one more time, it doesn't solve anything, and it only provides temporary relief.

When you want peace, what do you do? Work out? Go for a walk? Go shopping? Grab a coffee? If you're the mother of toddlers, then maybe you hide in the bathroom. Because those of us who have been there know that's the only place you can find to be alone and relish in a moment of peace and quiet . . . hopefully. List some things you turn to as you try to "find" peace.

As much as we might try and find peace anywhere in this world, these things will not last. Only one place will ever provide real peace. Real peace is only in Jesus.

Read Isaiah 9:6, where the prophet Isaiah speaks of Jesus long before He came to earth. List the four names that refer to Jesus.

1.

2.

3.

4.

Circle the last name that you wrote.

Notice that Jesus was called "Peace" long before He was born. He was also called Peace when He was born. When angels announced His birth to the universe, they said something I've never seen on a birth announcement.

> *Glory to God in the highest heaven, and peace on earth to people he favors!*
> LUKE 2:14

First, we experience peace *with* God.
Second, we experience the peace *of* God.

Let's define these two concepts. First, we experience peace with God when we become followers of Jesus and are *reconciled to God*. Reconciliation is the "bringing together of two parties that are estranged . . . a change of relationship, an exchange of antagonism for goodwill, enmity for friendship."[2]

But God proves his own love for us in that while we were still sinners, Christ died for us. How much more then, since we have now been justified by his blood, will we be saved through him from wrath. For if, while we were enemies, we were reconciled to God through the death of his Son, then how much more, having been reconciled, will we be saved by his life. And not only that, but we also boast in God through our Lord Jesus Christ, through whom we have now received this reconciliation.

ROMANS 5:8–11

When Jesus was crucified, buried, risen from the dead, and seated at the right hand of the Father, He secured peace with God for all who would believe in Him.

When did Jesus lead you to have "peace with God" in your own spiritual journey? What difference has peace with God made in your life?

Second, the peace *of* God is the peace Jesus took with Him everywhere on this earth. After bringing us peace with God, He makes this peace *of* God available for us every day.

Think again of peace as *shalom* like we defined earlier. Can you think of examples from the Gospels where Jesus brought peace to people?

How else does Jesus give peace? You can look at these scriptures for some ideas: John 14:27; 16:33; Philippians 4:6–7; and 2 Timothy 1:7.

I want you to write a prayer in the shaded box below based on the verses you just read today and insights you wrote. Make it something you say aloud to renew your mind (Romans 12:1–2).

Start with saying your name. That's what I do. "Christine," and off I go reminding myself aloud what the truth is, and what to think based on the Word. That's how I practice choosing my thoughts and having a healthy mind.

Do you feel any more peaceful? If not, then repeat your prayer. Treat it like shampoo: Rinse and repeat.

Isaiah 26:3 is a promise from God to me and to you for just this very thing. It's a verse we want to memorize and take to heart.

> *You will keep the mind that is dependent on you in perfect peace, for it is trusting in you.*
> ISAIAH 26:3

You can rinse and repeat this verse all day long, especially on days that feel like you're waging a minute-by-minute war in your mind and emotions. In those moments, stop and ask, "God, what potential outcome am I afraid of? What truth about who You are and what You do brings peace even if that outcome occurs?"

So, let's agree together to bring His peace. Let's post peace on social media and not contribute to the chaos. Let's speak peace to our friends when a diagnosis or divorce rocks their world. More than anything, I want Jesus' peace for them, and for you.

PRAY

Leader (or volunteer) read the prayer aloud, or pray independently over your group before closing your time together.

As we close out our time today, my prayer for you is that you walk in a greater understanding of God's peace and lean into it every single day.

Heavenly Father, I pray the peace that surpasses all understanding would guard our hearts and minds in Christ Jesus. That just like Philippians 4:8 says, we think on things that are true, honorable, just, pure, lovely, commendable, of moral excellence, and praiseworthy. That we lean into your peace every moment of every day. In Jesus' name, amen.

DAY 2 Finding Inner Peace

I was so relieved to see Julia and the rest of our Ukraine A21 team on our global Zoom call. War had broken out in Ukraine, and Julia was our country manager based in Kyiv. Our security team had guided them with their families to a safehouse via satellite. They were huddled together on a sofa where they took turns telling us what they had seen and experienced. Never in all the years of A21 had I witnessed such courage, such strength, and such faith in our team. When we got to the close of our meeting, Julia prayed, in the midst of leading her team, her children, and escaping to Poland while her husband was made to stay and fight for Ukraine.

"Lord . . . we are grateful for Your protection and provision, and for everything that You have already done, and everything You have prepared for us ahead. We trust You . . . we know You have so much for us as an organization here in Ukraine and globally . . . we are so grateful that we can be Your hands and Your feet to rescue people for freedom and restoration . . . keep our hearts that we would notice and see the miracles that You're doing around us. Thank You, Lord."

Julia's prayer brought us all a measure of God's peace and unity as we trusted Him. The circumstances, though, didn't get better. The war escalated, cities were decimated, innocent people were killed, and families were separated. Still, because of God, we had an inner peace that defied our understanding. At the end of our Zoom call, I stayed on as long as I could. Never had I felt so responsible and desperate for so many. As my tears spilled so did my prayers. How could I not cry my prayers?

"Lord, please be their refuge and their fortress. Cover them under Your wings. Protect them from any harm . . . have mercy on everyone in Ukraine."

If I didn't have the peace of God on the inside of me, I'd for sure be a mess trying to deal with what goes on in my outer world. Because peace is an inside-out affair. It's something that begins inside of us and radiates outward. If we do not have inner peace, then we won't have outward peace. And we will not be equipped to navigate the chaotic world around us.

Write about a situation where you had peace on the inside even though everything was chaotic on the outside.

When Paul wrote a letter to a church, he always included a greeting with the word peace. To the Romans . . . to the Corinthians . . . to the Galatians . . . to the Ephesians . . . to the Philippians . . . to the Colossians . . . to the Thessalonians . . . to Timothy . . . to Titus . . . to Philemon . . . he wrote, "grace to you and peace." Peace was clearly something they needed. Peace is clearly something we need, because so many things can steal our peace.

Look up the following verses and draw a line to the corresponding word mentioned in the verse that steals our peace.

ISAIAH 41:10	CONFUSION
MATTHEW 6:25–34	STRIFE/CONTENTION
1 CORINTHIANS 14:33	WORRY
ROMANS 12:18	DISAPPOINTMENT/DEPRESSION
PHILIPPIANS 4:6	FEAR
PSALM 42:5–6	ANXIOUSNESS
ISAIAH 61:3	SADNESS
JOHN 16:16, 20	GRIEF

Things steal our peace because we don't think we have control, but Scripture paints a much different picture.

Colossians 3:15 says, "And let the peace of Christ, to which you were also called in one body, rule your hearts. And be thankful."

Underline the word *let*.

Inner peace is something we let rule in our hearts. It might be hard, but this verse shows us it's possible.

Reread Philippians 4:6 and underline the first phrase of the verse.

Don't worry about anything, but in everything, through prayer and petition with thanksgiving, present your requests to God.
PHILIPPIANS 4:6

God told us to be anxious for nothing and not to worry about anything, so surely it's possible, right? Not convinced? I understand how this can be hard to comprehend. Stay with me. If we want peace in our world, but we're tied up in knots on the inside, then it's time to start untying our internal knots.

What is it that you're most stressed about right now? Write it here.

Can you do anything to change the situation? If not, write *nothing*. If so, list how.

If you wrote *nothing*, I have good news. Peace is possible whether your situation changes or not, because peace starts inside of you. It's not circumstance-dependent, but heart-condition-dependent.

Let's expand our understanding of Philippians 4:6 to include a few more verses. Philippians 4:4–7 tells us: "Rejoice in the Lord always. I will say it again: Rejoice! Let your graciousness be known to everyone. The Lord is near. Don't worry about anything, but in everything, through prayer and petition with thanksgiving, present your requests to God. And the peace of God, which surpasses all understanding, will guard your hearts and minds in Christ Jesus."

What are you thinking about? Put a star by every category that dominates your inner world more than God's peace. I left you some blank lines so you can list specific things.

THE PAST	MY MARRIAGE	BEING SINGLE	MY JOB
MY FAILURES	THE BILLS	SCHOOL/GRADES	MY KID(S)
MY DREAMS	CAREGIVING	TOMORROW	RETIREMENT

Our superpower is being a non-anxious presence in an anxious world. We become non-anxious in two ways: through prayer and the renewal of our minds, something we'll talk more about in Week 5. Through prayer, we take things to God and leave them there. And when we take something back, we return to leave it with God once more. First Peter 5:6–7 tells us to, "Humble yourselves, therefore, under the mighty hand of God, so that he may exalt you at the proper time, casting all your cares on him, because he cares about you."

How can we cast all our cares on Jesus? Write your ideas here.

Next, walk through the following steps to cast your cares, and exchange your anxiousness for God's peace.

1. Look back at what you wrote about a situation currently stressing you.
2. Go to God's Word and find a verse. Find a promise that addresses your situation.
3. Write that verse on sticky notes and put them where you'll consistently see them: on your dashboard, computer, mirror, coffee maker, or refrigerator. If you feel like you do endless loads of laundry, tape it to the front of your washer or dryer.
4. Make yourself think about that verse and say it more than you think and speak about the situation that is stealing your peace.

This is how we make the Bible and God's peace a reality in our lives with a chaotic world around us. Learning to do this on a consistent basis will help you respond with God's promises when a situation arises to steal your peace. You don't deny the reality, but you don't let it consume you, either. You lean into God and His peace. You let His Word and His peace be bigger in your thoughts than the threat to your peace.

PRAY

Leader (or volunteer) read the prayer aloud, or pray independently over your group before closing your time together.

Good job with the past two days of work. I hope you're finding peace as we go. Thank you for taking this journey with me. As we close out our day, my prayer for you is based on 2 Thessalonians 3:16.

May the Lord of peace Himself give you peace always in every way. The Lord be with all of you. In Jesus' name, amen.

DAY 3 Blessed Are the Peacemakers

When I first gave my life fully to God and started working with youth in my early twenties, I was passionate about Jesus and my work, but it was not something my family understood, nor did they celebrate with me that I had found a new path that meant so much to me. They saw my zeal for Jesus and youth work more as a passing phase that I'd outgrow or something. They certainly didn't expect me to be so "all in" that I'd stop going to the church where I grew up and start going somewhere else completely new, and yet, that's exactly what I did.

But a couple years later, when it became clear that ministry was going to be my forever path . . . that I was not going back to my corporate career path . . . that I loved working with youth in the nonprofit sector . . . well, what started as merely tension grew into constant conflict and arguing.

It was especially difficult when it came to my relationship with Mum. Because I lived at home, our differences of opinion were always front and center; there was no escaping it. Though she loved me dearly, she didn't have a framework in which to understand why I would want to go anywhere else to church, particularly after she and my dad had so faithfully raised my brothers and me in the church where all our extended family attended together. To Mum, it was even more: I wasn't just leaving the church; I was leaving her and all the dreams she had for my life. I can assure you that my Greek mother never envisioned her daughter entering into full time vocational ministry, and in her mind, throwing away her education, future, and hope of a flourishing life. How could I?

So, for days that turned into weeks, I got up every morning, went to work, and came home at the end of the day without her saying one word to me. That's how Mum handled it—with silence. She froze me out. For months. She was feisty and strong and determined in it all. And though I was as heartbroken as she was, I had no idea what to do to bridge the gap, to heal her pain, to heal my own, to make peace, to bring us back together. So, I practiced what I now know is avoidance. I avoided home as much as I could. I came in late at night after she was asleep, and we drifted relationally to being like two ships passing in the night. Until . . .

One day, I had a sense it was time to make peace, somehow, but the argument that ensued in my head held me back: She's the one being extremely unfair. She's the one who's unkind to me. She's the one who stopped talking to me. She was the one who was mean. But God wasn't giving me a pass.

He began ever so gently to lead me to go home sooner in the evenings. To offer her coffee while she was watching TV. To wash any dishes left in the sink at night before I went to bed. For the first few months, she'd shake her head no about the coffee. She wouldn't acknowledge the clean dishes. And she still didn't speak to me.

None of it was easy. I rarely liked it. In fact, most of the time, I dreaded it. It was awkward, uncomfortable, humiliating, and at times, it stirred more anger in me because of all the emotion I felt and didn't know how to work through. It took a long time for my feelings to catch up to my emotions. Sometimes, extending an olive branch to someone is hard, really, really, hard, because sometimes the other person doesn't reciprocate, and we have to make peace within ourselves and leave it at that.

With Mum, I kept doing what I felt God wanted me to do. Night after night, I'd get home, sit with her while she watched her soap operas, offer her coffee, and, eventually, go into the kitchen, and with tears streaming down my face, I'd wash all the dishes.

Finally, there came a night when I offered her coffee, and she spoke. She said, "Yes." That was all, but that was enough. The ice was thawing, if just a little. It took a while for us to actually begin rebuilding our relationship, but we both moved one baby step closer to the other little by little, day by day. It was truly the beginning of us building a real mother/daughter relationship—one where we found the middle ground, one where we mutually admired one another and interacted as adults. When we finally got there, it was more than either of us ever thought possible. We loved, laughed, and talked almost daily about everything that went on in our lives. When I married, she even walked me down the aisle, though I had to convince her that God would be okay with it. And when Nick and I had our girls, she lit up at being their Yia Yia. As she aged and I eventually had to let her go, the grief was overwhelming. I knew that she loved me before she ever knew me, and I loved her for it.

Making peace with my mum felt like a crash course in learning to become a *peacemaker*, but little did I know that God was teaching me far more than I realized. What I learned and did to extend an olive branch to her wouldn't just apply to our relationship. It would apply to relationships throughout my life—because being a *peacemaker*, particularly in times of relational ***conflict*** and ***strife***, is something God has called us all to be.

Conflict usually stresses the action of forces in opposition but in static applications implies an irreconcilability as of duties or desires.[1]

Strife emphasizes a struggle for superiority rather than the incongruity or incompatibility of the persons or things involved.[2]

Conflict and **Strife**. These two words capture part of why we need to know how to be peacemakers. In light of these two words and their definitions, James poses an interesting question: "What causes fights and quarrels among you?"

Read James 4:1–10 and write his answer to this question.

In Matthew 5:9, Jesus said, "Blessed are the peacemakers, for they will be called sons of God."

Notice that last phrase. As Christ followers, we are sons and daughters of the King. We are grafted into His family. Though this verse says sons, it's speaking about everyone who comes to Christ, male or female, being a child of God—about being an heir instead of a slave, about being given rights and privileges—all because of our faith in Jesus (Galatians 4:1–7). If we're peacemakers, then in this context we're called sons of God—and that's a good thing!

Biblically, a *peacemaker* is someone "who actively works to bring about peace and reconciliation where there is hatred and enmity. God blesses peacemakers."[3]

Jesus spoke again to our being a peacemaker in the same chapter as the Beatitudes. Matthew 5:23–24 says, "So if you are offering your gift on the altar, and there you remember that your brother or sister has something against you, leave your gift there in front of the altar. First go and be reconciled with your brother or sister, and then come and offer your gift."

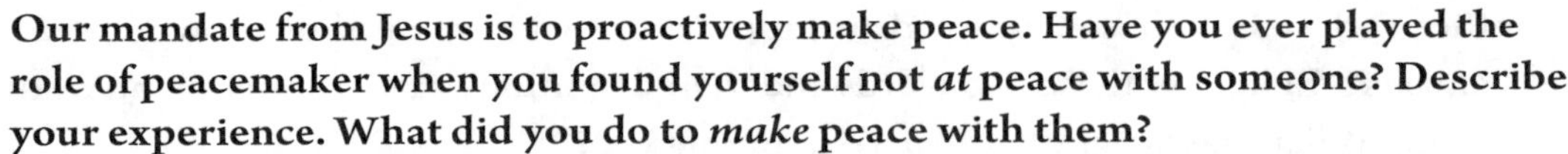

Our mandate from Jesus is to proactively make peace. Have you ever played the role of peacemaker when you found yourself not *at* peace with someone? Describe your experience. What did you do to *make* peace with them?

Was the person you made peace with receptive to your peacemaking? Describe how their reaction made you feel.

One of the hardest things for any of us to accept is when someone doesn't want to make peace with us, even after we've done all we know to do to extend an olive branch. I have a few of those relationships in my life. I've come to realize that if we live long enough, we get them, even if we do everything we can not to have them. I do my best and take to heart what Paul wrote in Romans 12:18: "If possible, as far as it depends on you, live at peace with everyone."

If you have someone who won't make peace, despite doing all you can to be a peacemaker, how have you managed it? In your emotions? In your thought life? In your actions? In your prayers? In your posts? Ouch, I know. How many times do we take to social media to post our opinions in times of discord? Is that really the place to air our differences? I realize it's common in this day and age, but is that a viable way to be a peacemaker?

Write your responses to the questions in that last paragraph here.

In my life, when I've tried to make peace with someone who hasn't really wanted the same, I've had to find peace in doing what I knew I had the power to do for that person, then commit that person to God. It's one of the hardest things for me, but I've found that it's all any of us can do.

I've also found that sometimes people will seem to be willing to make peace, be at peace, and keep the peace, when there is really no peace. I would call this a relational conflict where there may not be verbal disagreement, but it certainly feels like you can cut the air with a knife when you're around them. Do you have someone in your life like this? They're the person with whom you walk on eggshells when you're around them.

Keeping the peace brings a false kind of peace temporarily. I imagine we've all done this to stave off an argument, postpone a conversation we're not ready to have, or to avoid conflict all together. But it doesn't bring the kind of lasting peace Jesus gives us, which is true peace.

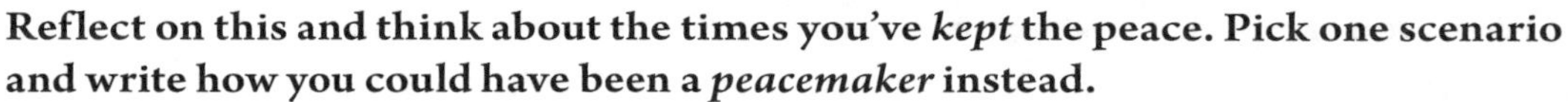

Reflect on this and think about the times you've *kept* the peace. Pick one scenario and write how you could have been a *peacemaker* instead.

It's critical that we learn how to make real peace. (If you want to *dig deeper*, look up each of the following verses and write any strategies you find that God wants us to have as peacemakers: Matthew 7:3–5; 18:15–17, 21–22.)

I have found that to grow as peacemakers we're going to have to be honest—with ourselves and with others. We're going to have to keep developing our communication skills so they're healthy, truthful, and kind—because God wants peacemaking to be an ongoing part of our lives. Even when we run into people who seem to come alive in the chaos of not having peace.

PRAY

Leader (or volunteer) read the prayer aloud, or pray independently over your group before closing your time together.

Being a peacemaker is being obedient to God. It's something He's called us to be, equipped us to be, and given us a heart to be, particularly as we develop His character in our lives. But it's not always easy. Sometimes it's gut-wrenching and soaked in tears, especially when it doesn't go the way we hoped.

As we close out our day, my prayer for you is based on Luke 6:31 . . . "Just as you want others to do for you, do the same for them."

Heavenly Father, help us to remember the Golden Rule based on Your Word. Help us to remember to treat others the way we want to be treated, to do to them and for them the way we want things to be done to and for us. Help us to be peacemakers who make peace, spread peace, and initiate peace everywhere we go and everywhere we post. In Jesus' name, amen.

DAY 4 Flip Some Tables

When I first began to speak about the reality of human trafficking in Greece, I encountered resistance. This surprised me because some accounts have estimated that Greece's border with Turkey serves as the "back door" for close to ninety percent of the illegal immigrants to the European Union, including those transported for sexual exploitation.[1] Bringing this injustice to light to set people free, bring justice to traffickers, and dismantle unjust systems was a no-brainer to me, but not everyone saw it this way.

After several years of raising awareness, many organizations and churches across Greece, and around the world, thankfully came on board to support the work of A21. Just recently, we saw fifty-two young women identified and assisted out of sex trafficking in Greece and twenty traffickers captured in one raid. A friend who knows me all too well said to me, "Chris, you had to flip some tables and disturb the status quo to wake people up to the reality of human trafficking in our country, but look at what the Lord has done."

At the time of writing this Bible study, A21 is eighteen years old with teams serving in nineteen offices in fourteen countries who have reached more than fifteen million people with prevention, awareness, or education. We have answered thousands of calls, helping to identify and assist thousands of victims. We have won more than one-hundred-fifty criminal court cases and trained thousands of frontline professionals. And we're just getting started!

To be peacemakers, we sometimes have to acknowledge that there is no peace. We have to face what we don't want to face. We sometimes need to disrupt the status quo, the false peace of the comfortable and complacent. We have to disturb this "peace" as the Old Testament prophets of God did. Jeremiah prophesied that judgment was coming on Jerusalem, while the false prophets claimed "peace." Ezekiel spoke similar warnings. Both prophets used a particular phrase as they exposed the lies of the false prophets.

Look up the following verses and write the phrase they have in common. It might sound familiar.

JEREMIAH 6:14

EZEKIEL 13:16

Today this phrase, "peace, peace, when there is no peace," is used when we prefer comfort and the status quo in our relationships, workplaces, or communities. But Jesus wants us to be free and to know true peace. He wants us to pursue and bring true peace into situations everywhere, and that might mean disrupting a false sense of peace. The same Jesus who said, "Blessed are the peacemakers" (Matthew 5:9), also had to disrupt the peace so He could bring about peace.

Have you ever heard the phrase "flip some tables" used the way my friend did? It refers to Jesus going into the temple and turning over the tables of those who were using God's house for unholy purposes. In our vernacular, it refers to standing up for something or someone by disrupting the status quo. "Flipping some tables" means disturbing the false peace that people have wrongly accepted.

All four gospels give similar accounts of Jesus flipping the tables. Read it in Mark 11:15–18 and fill in the blanks.

They came to Jerusalem, and he went into the temple and began to ________________ ________ those buying and selling. He ____________________ the tables of the money changers and the chairs of those selling doves, and would not permit anyone to carry goods through the temple. He was teaching them: "Is it not written, 'My house will be called a house of prayer for all nations'? But you have made it a den of thieves!" The chief priests and the scribes heard it and started looking for a way to kill him. For they were afraid of him, because the whole crowd was astonished by his teaching.

MARK 11:15–18

Jesus had a table-flipping side. Luke 12:49 quotes Jesus as saying, "I came to bring fire on the earth, and how I wish it were already set ablaze!" Yes, Jesus came to save, heal, and teach, but He didn't come to play! At times we need to act like Jesus—in more than the ways we find comfortable and appealing.

Can you think of times when you've had to flip a few tables and disturb the peace to initiate change where change needed to take place? Circle the ones that apply to you and your experiences. If you think of more, use the blank spaces and write in your additions.

IN YOUR MARRIAGE	AT YOUR WORK
IN YOUR EXTENDED FAMILY RELATIONSHIPS	AT YOUR CHILDREN'S SCHOOL
IN YOUR COMMUNITY	IN YOUR PARENTING
IN YOUR FRIENDSHIPS	IN YOUR OWN SELF-CARE

Maybe you initiated a necessary change that affected more people than you ever expected. If you did, then describe what your actions accomplished.

When we identify something that needs to change, we might have to initiate the change. One way we can do this is found in Ephesians 4:15: "But speaking the truth in love, let us grow in every way into him who is the head—Christ."

In your own words, define what "speaking the truth in love" means.

Have you ever had to speak the truth in love and confront someone, so that there could be genuine peace and not false peace?

I have found that *tone* and *timing* are just as important to speaking the truth in love as actually telling the truth. Nick often says, "Chris, it's not what you say, it's how you say it."

When it comes to timing, if I want Nick or one of my girls to hear me, the minute they walk in the door is probably not the right time. It can take great restraint to wait, to sit on something I desperately want to point out. Over the years I've learned the best time to tell Nick something and the best time to tell my girls something. And believe me, it's not late at night, or after an exhausting day, or when they're stressed or hungry! They have learned to do the same for me. If you have something to tell me, give me a cup of coffee first. It will really help my receptivity!

Pick the right time. Say it with the right tone. Tell the truth.

This is speaking the truth in love. The word *love* in Ephesians 4:15 is *agape*, "a self-sacrificial love that works for the benefit of the loved one."[2] Rather than unloading to make ourselves feel better, our purpose should be loving service led by prayer and the Holy Spirit.

Speaking the truth in love includes confronting ourselves where we need to be confronted. It's easier to call someone else out, but we need to do the painful work of flipping the tables in our own hearts and minds, too.

Can you identify within yourself places of denial that you need to call out—if to no one else but to yourself and God?

What steps can you take this week to create real peace in that area of your life?

PRAY

Leader (or volunteer) read the prayer aloud, or pray independently over your group before closing your time together.

My prayer for you today is based on a good reminder from Matthew's Gospel: "First take the beam of wood out of your eye, and then you will see clearly to take the splinter out of your brother's eye" (Matthew 7:5).

Heavenly Father, thank You for teaching us how to flip tables first starting with our own hearts. Help us to disturb our own false peace to bring forth true peace. Then, help us to practice this kind of justice in our world. To stand up for what's right with humility and compassion. To speak with truth and gentleness. In Jesus' name, amen.

DAY 5 Guided Prayer and Journaling

But I am like a flourishing olive tree in the house of God;
I trust in God's faithful love forever and ever.

PSALM 52:8

In my journey of following God, I've learned to keep as many things as simple as possible. The simpler I keep my life in this very complex world, the more peace I have. So, every now and then, I find it's good to declutter my heart and my mind. To take an inventory of what I'm carrying around—spiritually, mentally, emotionally, and even physically. Have I made it all harder than I need to? What have I given my peace of mind over to?

I've often found that being out in nature helps me with this, whether walking on a beach, lying on a hammock, or climbing a mountain in the world God made. Such things help me find a more peaceful order in my mind. The slower pace gives me a whole new perspective.

For example, when I started hiking, I had no idea how it would serve to fuel my passion for keeping life simple. I discovered that when I reach a summit, there is a kind of peace like no other that comes over me. Even gasping and desperate to sit down and rest, I can't escape standing in awe of God's overwhelming greatness. My mind can't help but rest on Him.

When I take in the sweeping 360-degree view, I have no doubt there is a supernatural peace available to us. It defies my understanding. Whatever I might have been dealing with at the start of any trailhead—problems to solve, relationships to resolve, issues to sort—seems replaced by what matters more—my peace of mind that comes from trusting in and depending on God and God alone.

Isaiah 26:3 encourages us saying, "You will keep the mind that is dependent on you in perfect peace, for it is trusting in you."

Today is our journaling and prayer day, so let's spend some time decluttering our hearts and minds. Let's invite Jesus in to help us sort through what's taking up space in our heads, so we have perfect peace.

Where are you wrestling with trusting God more? Identify the clutter standing in your way—things stealing your peace.

Past events you cannot change?

Situations you have yet to process?

Wounds that haven't healed?

A relationship calling you to be a peacemaker?

A child that seems far from God?

A financial mountain that seems insurmountable?

A medical challenge that feels ominous?

Write that one big thing weighing on your mind today.

Take what comes to mind to Jesus and lay it at His feet. Spend time with Him. Sit in the quiet, listening for truth, resting in His love.

I have come to understand that the kind of peace Jesus bought for us is not the absence of problems, but the presence of Jesus Himself.

When you're finished, journal about your experience with Him here.

WEEK 4

Oil from Pressing

GROUP STUDY

Watch

Watch the video for Week 4: Oil from Pressing, recording your thoughts as you listen.

Though God doesn't cause them, what if the most crushing and painful seasons of our lives are precisely what He uses to produce something valuable and beautiful in us?

Difficult, painful, and "crushing" experiences are often the very means by which God develops our character and faith.

God does not waste our pain. He uses life's pressures to press out bitterness, pride, and self-reliance, and to produce Christlike character within us.

> *Messiah* (Hebrew) and *Christ* (Greek) both mean the "Anointed One."[1]

Olive oil was the fuel that kept lamps burning, symbolizing spiritual readiness and our call to be a light in the darkness.

The oil represents our personal, daily relationship with God—our spiritual preparedness. It cannot be borrowed or bought at the last minute. We must cultivate our own supply.

> *"The wise ones, however, took oil in jars along with their lamps."*
> MATTHEW 25:4 NIV

Discuss

Leader (or volunteer), read the following aloud to the group and follow with the prompts for discussion.

After olives are harvested, they are quickly cleaned and crushed into a paste, pits and all. In some methods, the paste is spread onto fibrous cloths and layered one on top of the other, then pressed with even more intense pressure so that every drop of oil is squeezed out.[2] The best-tasting olive oil is made from this process of perfectly timed picking, weighted crushing, intense pressing, heating, cooling, and finally bottling.

We are asked to reframe our struggles within this powerful metaphor: Like the olive, God uses life's pressures to produce something of incredible value in and from us.

How does this perspective challenge or affirm the way you have viewed difficult seasons in your life?

Share about a "pressing" time that, in hindsight, you can see God used to produce Christ-like character or strength in you.

The name Gethsemane (*Gat Shemanim* in Hebrew) means oil press.[3] This was the place of Jesus' greatest agony and ultimate surrender to the Father's will.

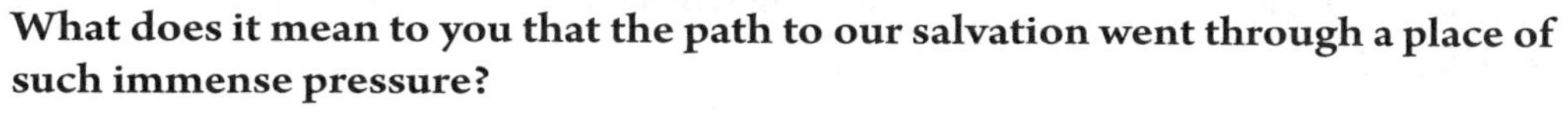

What does it mean to you that the path to our salvation went through a place of such immense pressure?

How does Christ's example in the garden encourage you when you face your own Gethsemane moments of decision and surrender?

In the Old Testament, anointing with oil signified that someone was set apart and empowered for God's specific purpose. Jesus is the ultimate "Anointed One" (Messiah/Christ), empowered by the Spirit for His mission.

As followers of Christ, we are also anointed by the Holy Spirit. In what specific area of your life do you need to be reminded that you have been set apart and divinely empowered for God's purpose?

But you have an anointing from the Holy One, and all of you know the truth. . . . As for you, the anointing you received from him remains in you, and you don't need anyone to teach you. Instead, his anointing teaches you about all things and is true and is not a lie; just as it has taught you, remain in him.

1 JOHN 2:20, 27

How does knowing you have an anointing from God give you confidence to live out your faith?

The Parable of the Ten Virgins (Matthew 25:1–13) illustrates spiritual readiness, where the oil represents our personal, daily cultivation of a relationship with God. The parable shows that spiritual readiness cannot be borrowed at the last minute.

What are the practical, daily habits you can cultivate to "keep your lamp full of oil"?

If we're going to run our race so that we obtain the prize, which is Jesus, then we will have to press on. We must press through everything that is pressing on us and against us . . . through our feelings, ambitions, expectations, and, yes, successes, which oftentimes cause us to fall into apathy or arrogance. This might mean that we will have to press play, pause, or stop in certain areas or seasons of our lives—so that we can live like flourishing olive trees in the house of God.

Our challenge then is to shift our question from "Why is this happening?" to "God, what are you trying to produce in me through this?"

What specific pressure point are you facing right now where you can apply this change in perspective?

How can this group pray for you as you seek to see God's purpose in your current pressures?

GROW

Consider these responses to what you've seen and heard today.

- Take Philippians 3:12–14 and make it your own anthem of faith—to use now and in the future as you go through crushing times and press in on your faith, to grow through the circumstance, not just go through it. Memorize it and begin using it in prayer as a declaration to God.

Not that I have already reached the goal or am already perfect, but I make every effort to take hold of it because I also have been taken hold of by Christ Jesus. Brothers and sisters, I do not consider myself to have taken hold of it. But one thing I do: Forgetting what is behind and reaching forward to what is ahead, I pursue as my goal the prize promised by God's heavenly call in Christ Jesus.
PHILIPPIANS 3:12–14

PRAY

Leader (or volunteer) read the prayer aloud, or pray independently over your group before closing your time together.

Heavenly Father, in everything I face, I choose to press on—to grow through everything life throws my way. I pray that I walk as more than a conqueror in Christ Jesus (Romans 8:37), remembering that You are greater in me than the enemy I face (1 John 4:4). In Jesus' name I pray, amen.

NOTES

WEEK 4 | Oil from Pressing

PERSONAL STUDY

The steady rhythm of daily devotion is a vital part of flourishing in your life with Jesus. Set aside time this week to really dig into God's Word. Each day, open yourself up to the Spirit's work in your heart and mind. Then, prayerfully reflect on the beautiful truth He is revealing during this season of new growth.

DAY 1
Anointing

DAY 2
Lamps

DAY 3
Symbolic of the Holy Spirit

DAY 4
Liquid Gold

DAY 5
Guided Prayer and Journaling

DAY 1 Anointing

I have always had a soft spot in my heart for Queen Elizabeth II. I mean, I did grow up in Australia which is part of the Commonwealth, and her picture was on our five dollar bill. I also liked the way she loved her corgis. I became obsessed with the Netflix series *The Crown*, so I was so happy when Catherine was in college and decided to enroll in a study abroad program in London. Unfortunately, one day after landing in London to study, Catherine called to tell me that the nation was in mourning because Queen Elizabeth had died at ninety-six years old. We were all so sad. Of course, I could not miss watching the coronation of King Charles III.

I remember watching the coronation and being totally excited not only at all the pomp and pageantry, but also that it included Greek Orthodox music as a tribute to Prince Philip, King Charles' father who was born in Greece.[1] What can I say? I'm Greek!

What I was especially drawn to during the coronation, particularly in light of our study this week, was when the Archbishop of Canterbury anointed King Charles. You couldn't see it, because of the screens placed around the king, concealing him from view, but behind the cloth, the archbishop anointed the king's hands, breast and head with holy oil—which was olive oil. And not just any olive oil.

The olive oil, or chrism as it's referred to for the coronation, was produced out of olives from groves on the Mount of Olives—the same place where Jesus prayed in the Garden of Gethsemene. According to Buckingham Palace, the olive oil for King Charles' coronation was consecrated in Jerusalem and based on the same ingredients as the oil used in the 1953 coronation of Queen Elizabeth—a formula which has been used for hundreds of years.[2]

Though Charles became king the moment his mother passed away, anointing him as king is a symbolic religious rite. And the coronation ceremony, which includes the anointing, signifies the transfer of the monarch's title and authority as the official head of the Church of England.[3]

I find it fascinating that not only has olive oil been used to anoint kings and queens for centuries, but it also has been used for such anointings since biblical times. There are literally references to anointing people, places, and things all throughout the Bible in both the Old and New Testaments.

In the Old Testament, anointing signified consecration, being made sacred and holy, whether for people, animals, or objects. For people, it involved a ritual of pouring or smearing oil on a person's head or forehead.[4]

You prepare a table before me in the presence of my enemies; you anoint my head with oil;
my cup overflows.
PSALM 23:5

Anoint

The Hebrew verb for *anoint* (*mashach*) "refers to the spreading or smearing of a liquid. . . . Anointing in the Bible signifies that God was staking a claim on the anointed and/or that God was pouring out His Spirit upon the anointed."[5]

Anointing often installed someone in a new office or role of authority. The Bible contains examples of three types of people who were anointed:

1. Kings (1 Samuel 10:1; 16:12–13; 1 Kings 19:15–16)
2. Priests (Exodus 28:41; Leviticus 8:12)
3. Prophets (1 Kings 19:15–16)

In the Old Testament, sacrifices were also anointed. Read the following verses and jot a note to the side as to what kind of sacrifice it was . . . for example, an animal or a grain.

"Sacrifice a bull as a sin offering each day for atonement. Purify the altar when you make atonement for it, and anoint it in order to consecrate it."
EXODUS 29:36

"If he presents it for thanksgiving, in addition to the thanksgiving sacrifice, he is to present unleavened cakes mixed with olive oil, unleavened wafers coated with oil, and well-kneaded cakes of fine flour mixed with oil."
LEVITICUS 7:12

In other translations, being coated with oil reads as being smeared with oil, which we've already learned is being anointed with oil (see ESV, NET).

In addition to people and sacrifices, objects were also anointed. God told Moses, "Take the anointing oil and anoint the tabernacle and everything in it; consecrate it along with all its furnishings so that it will be holy. Anoint the altar of burnt offering and all its utensils; consecrate the altar so that it will be especially holy. Anoint the basin and its stand and consecrate it" (Exodus 40:9–11).

Turning to the New Testament, we find that Jesus Himself was anointed—but not exactly like we see in the Old Testament.

To start, one of the most beautiful moments at the beginning of Jesus' earthly ministry was when He entered the synagogue in Nazareth and read from the scroll of Isaiah . . . about Himself. He stood up to read and once He finished, He told the people that what Isaiah wrote was fulfilled in Him.

> *The Spirit of the Lord is on me, because he has anointed me to preach good news to the poor. He has sent me to proclaim release to the captives and recovery of sight to the blind, to set free the oppressed, to proclaim the year of the Lord's favor.*
> LUKE 4:18–19

Who anointed Jesus in this text?

What do you think the anointing did for Jesus?

Jesus is the "anointed one." The term *messiah* (Greek: *Christos*) literally means "anointed one."[6] Though not always literally with oil, as Jesus was anointed with the Holy Spirit. As Messiah, He was anointed from the beginning; He was anointed for ministry; and He was anointed near the end of His life.

Throughout the New Testament, anointing is associated with the burial of Jesus, as well as healing and the celebration of meals. For example, James 5:14 tells us, "Is anyone among you sick? He should call for the elders of the church, and they are to pray over him, anointing him with oil in the name of the Lord."

Churches today still practice anointing with symbolic meaning, often during ceremonies of consecration, or prayers of dedication, or healing. Are you aware of ways that anointing might be used in your church? Jot a list here.

Have you ever been a part of a gathering that used anointing oil in the way James instructed above? Describe your experience here.

Have you ever used it as part of your personal spiritual practices? Describe the purpose for which you used it and why.

I've been known to carry olive oil in a little bottle in my purse from time to time. It's my way of being ready to pray for anyone, anytime, anywhere.

PRAY

Leader (or volunteer) read the prayer aloud, or pray independently over your group before closing your time together.

As we close out our day, my prayer for you is that just as Jesus was anointed to preach the good news to the poor, to proclaim freedom to captives, recovery of sight to the blind, to set the oppressed free, and to declare the year of the Lord's favor, we, too, carry out His mission.

Heavenly Father, help us go into every day with faith, prayer, and compassion, doing the work You've called us to do. Lead us to divine appointments where we can preach the good news to those who are poor spiritually. Help us show people the way to freedom in You. And in our encouragement, help those blind spiritually to see and those oppressed to be lifted up. Direct us to the people who need us most. In Jesus' name, amen.

DAY 2 Lamps

When Sophia was barely school age, she went through this phase of being utterly captivated by flashlights. She had little ones, big ones, colorful ones, and themed ones covered in her favorite characters. She carried them in her backpack, her purse, and her luggage. She kept one on her nightstand, one under her pillow, and one under the bed. She even taped one to the handlebar on her bike so she could have a headlight. Suffice it to say that if we wanted to play a game of flashlight tag, we were more than covered.

With the bigger flashlights, Sophia loved putting her little hand on top and staring at the pinky-orange glow that illuminated her fingers. At night, after she was settled in bed, she'd shine a flashlight across the ceiling, making swirls and designs with her imagination.

But no matter how many flashlights Sophia collected, she always wanted one more. I'll never forget one night racing through Walmart, gathering up supplies, and heading for the checkout, when she spied a four-sided display loaded with flashlights, all new designs and colors she apparently didn't possess and didn't want to live without. When she asked for one, though she had plenty at home, I couldn't resist. She'd been so good all day and not complained once as Nick and I had run so many errands. Besides, I knew there'd come a day when she'd outgrow such a phase.

Carefully—and slowly I might add—she examined each and every one before making her choice. When she did, she picked it up, switched it on, and cupped her little hands around it in desperation to see how bright it was. Of course, the giant fluorescent lighting in the store made it next to impossible to see, so Nick cupped his hands around it to try and create enough glow for her solidify her choice.

Once Sophia was confident that she'd picked the right one, we went to the checkout to pay, and she said something I have absolutely never forgotten: "Oh Mummy, can we please go find some darkness?"

I've never forgotten because it just arrested my attention, right then and there in the store. Sophia meant it innocently, because she wanted to see how bright her new flashlight was. But to my ear, it was much more.

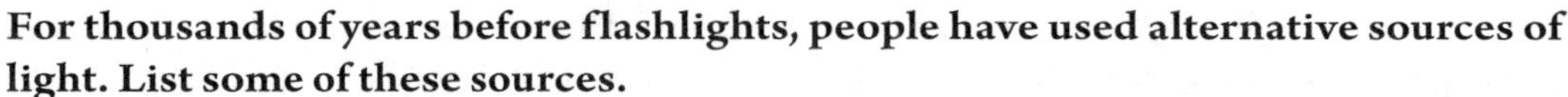

For thousands of years before flashlights, people have used alternative sources of light. List some of these sources.

As recently as a century ago, people commonly used oil lamps made of glass. Maybe you've seen one in an antique store. The earliest lamps were nothing more than a stone or clay bowl filled with olive oil or animal fat and a wick made of twisted plant fibers.[1] The wick would draw up the oil or fat so it could burn and provide light. During the time of Jesus, potters made small clay lamps that burned olive oil. The lamps were placed in homes in niches in the wall or on stands.

While we know that God created light when He formed the world, the first mention of a lamp is found after God gives Moses specific instructions for the first high priest, Aaron, and the tent of meeting.

Read Exodus 37:17–24 and write the description of lamp/lampstand. If you like to draw, sketch an image based on the description.

Read Exodus 27:20 or Leviticus 24:1–4 and note what kind of oil was to be used in the cups of the lampstand in the temple.

Notice that the cups on the lampstand were to be kept *full* of oil so that they would burn continuously and not go out, and that it was Aaron's job to tend to them.

In the New Testament, Jesus told a parable that mentions something similar to this. Read the account from Matthew 25:1–13 and answer the questions that follow.

> *"At that time the kingdom of heaven will be like ten virgins who took their lamps and went out to meet the groom. Five of them were foolish and five were wise. When the foolish took their lamps, they didn't take oil with them; but the wise ones took oil in their flasks with their lamps. When the groom was delayed, they all became drowsy and fell asleep.*
>
> *"In the middle of the night there was a shout: 'Here's the groom! Come out to meet him.'*
>
> *"Then all the virgins got up and trimmed their lamps. The foolish ones said to the wise ones, 'Give us some of your oil, because our lamps are going out.'*
>
> *"The wise ones answered, 'No, there won't be enough for us and for you. Go instead to those who sell oil, and buy some for yourselves.'*
>
> *"When they had gone to buy some, the groom arrived, and those who were ready went in with him to the wedding banquet, and the door was shut. Later the rest of the virgins also came and said, 'Master, master, open up for us!'*
>
> *"He replied, 'Truly I tell you, I don't know you!'*
>
> *"Therefore be alert, because you don't know either the day or the hour."*
>
> MATTHEW 25:1–13

Underline the phrase in the first line that says, "will be like." This phrase helps us identify that this is a parable—a story told to teach us something.

What about this story might remind us of Aaron tending to the lampstand in the temple?

In the parable, the bridegroom represents Jesus, and the virgins represent Christians who await His return. The wise virgins, with the lamps and extra oil, were those who were prepared and ready for Jesus' return, while the foolish virgins were those who failed to prepare.

In our lives today, how can we keep being those with lamps burning, as those who are preparing and ready for Jesus' return?

Readying and preparing for Christ's return has personal impact, as well as present and eternal impact. Let's consider more of what God tells us about this theme.

Read the following verses and underline key words like *light, lamp, illuminates,* and *darkness.* (You can also *dig deeper* with John 12:46 and 1 John 1:5.)

> *Lord, you light my lamp; my God illuminates my darkness.*
> PSALM 18:28
>
> *Jesus spoke to them again: "I am the light of the world. Anyone who follows me will never walk in the darkness but will have the light of life."*
> JOHN 8:12
>
> *But you are a chosen race, a royal priesthood, a holy nation, a people for his possession, so that you may proclaim the praises of the one who called you out of darkness into his marvelous light.*
> 1 PETER 2:9

God gave us light when He hung the sun, moon, and stars in the sky. He told Moses that the lamps in the temple should be filled with oil so they could burn continuously. Jesus told the disciples about the ten virgins and their lamps so that they too would be ready with their lamps full of oil. Jesus told His disciples that He was the light of the world, and then He told them that they were the light of the world as well.

Read Matthew 5:14–16 and fill in the blanks:

"You are the the____________________ of the world. A city situated on a hill cannot be hidden. No one lights a ____________________ and puts it under a basket, but rather on a ____________________, and it gives __________________ for all who are in the house. In the same way, __________ ______________ ____________________ __________________ before others, so that they may ____________________ your ____________ __________ and _______________ ______________________ to your Father in heaven."

MATTHEW 5:14–16

Jesus said, "I am the light of the world," (John 8:12), and He said to His disciples, "You are the light of the world" (Matthew 5:14). Jesus wasn't contradicting Himself but showing the progression of giving ourselves to Him fully. First, His light floods our souls and swallows up all the darkness, and then we, too, become the light of the world. His light illuminates our darkness and shines brightly through us to others so they can see our good works and give our heavenly Father glory.

How can you allow the light of world—Jesus—to shine even more brightly through you?

We are called to be light everywhere we go, shining the light of Jesus in the darkness that we encounter each and every day. With words of life, encouragement, and truth, with actions of kindness, selflessness, and thoughtfulness, we shine so people give their lives to Jesus and give Him glory.

First Thessalonians 5:5 tells us, "For you are all children of light." Let's live like who God made us to be—the light of Jesus sent to our world.

PRAY

Leader (or volunteer) read the prayer aloud, or pray independently over your group before closing your time together.

As we come to the close of our day, my prayer for you is based on Ephesians 5:8–10: "For you were once darkness, but now you are light in the Lord. Walk as children of light— for the fruit of the light consists of all goodness, righteousness, and truth—testing what is pleasing to the Lord."

Heavenly Father, help us all walk as children of the light, bearing fruit that consists of all goodness, righteousness, and truth. Help us shine bright with Your light, dispelling all the darkness, everywhere we go and with everyone we meet. In Jesus' name, amen.

DAY 3 Symbolic of the Holy Spirit

Have you ever had a friend step in and help you in a moment when you needed it most? I have. More than once. And while some of the stories I could share would involve gut-wrenching life experiences and deep-seated emotions, there's one story that comes to mind that wasn't exactly a life or death moment, but it sure felt like it at the time. It happened on a day trip when I was hiking up Mount Baden-Powell, one of California's tallest peaks in the San Gabriel Mountains. The trail to the top is an eight-mile round trip that takes about five hours to hike,[1] and much like all the trails in Southern California, it has a warning sign at the trailhead alerting you to what's ahead, namely, "Beware of Rattlesnakes."

My friend and hiking buddy Dawn was with me that day, and in fact, was leading the way. Knowing how anxious I get at even the thought of encountering a snake on a trail, she typically walks ahead of me, prodding the bushes on either side of the path with her trekking pole. Dawn has been more than gracious to take on this role of "chief snake scarer."

On this particular day not all went according to plan when a giant rattlesnake outsmarted her—and he raced across the trail right in front of me. To this day, I'm not sure what happened, but I saw the rattlesnake, panicked, ran ahead flinging my poles, tripped and fell, pulled a calf muscle, bruised my arm, and seriously wasn't sure I'd be able to get off the mountain.

I do remember that after all the commotion I was on the ground nursing my leg, trying to get my calf muscle to relax, to let go and let me walk, but it was locked up. I was in so much pain that I was no longer afraid of the snake, since he was long gone, but now I was afraid I'd have to be airlifted off the mountain.

Had it not been for Dawn to help me calm down, hydrate, eat a snack, and get my head back in the right space, I'm not sure I would have kept going or even been able to. Because of her help, I was able to eventually stand up, put weight on my leg, and start to hobble forward.

Not only was Dawn there when I needed her most that day, she has taught me everything I need to know about hiking trails up mountains, across valleys, through forests, up rivers, and in desert climates. She's shared so much knowledge with me about what I need to eat, drink, wear, and pack. I could have never hiked all the trails I've trekked without her knowledge; she's been an immense help to me. Besides, of all she's taught me, one of the most important lessons is to never hike alone, and my almost-encounter with that rattlesnake was a good reminder as to why.

From my experience and from what I read in the Word, God never intended for any of us to do life without help. Before leaving this earth, Jesus told His disciples that they would need help to do all that He was calling them to do . . . and then He promised to provide the help they needed—the help that we need too.

In the NASB, John 15:26–27 says, "When the Helper comes, whom I will send to you from the Father, namely, the Spirit of truth who comes from the Father, He will testify about Me, and you are testifying as well, because you have been with Me from the beginning."

God is a *Trinity*, one God in three persons—Father, Son (Jesus Christ), and Holy Spirit. And of all the titles that Jesus could have ascribed to the third person of the Trinity, He calls the Holy Spirit, "Helper!"

If God knew that we would need help (and He did), and if God has made that help available (as He has), let's make much of the help He gives us by growing in our knowledge and relationship with our Helper—the Holy Spirit!

The Holy Spirit

In the Greek, the Holy Spirit's name is *paraklētos*. It means "advocate; helper or; intercessor."[2]

In the legal world, an *advocate* is "a person who acts as a spokesperson or representative of someone else's policy, purpose, or cause; especially before a judge in a court of law.[3]

It is the same in the biblical sense. The Holy Spirit is our advocate. We see this in John 14–16 and 1 John 2:1.[4]

The following show us more of what the Holy Spirit does.

"But the Counselor, the Holy Spirit, whom the Father will send in my name, will teach you all things and remind you of everything I have told you."
JOHN 14:26

> *"When the Spirit of truth comes, he will guide you into all the truth. For he will not speak on his own, but he will speak whatever he hears. He will also declare to you what is to come."*
> **JOHN 16:13**

What promises! It's so good to know that the Holy Spirit is not only in us (Romans 8:11), but also with us to help us know whatever it is that we need to know.

The Holy Spirit's role in helping us walk in God's will and fulfill God's plans and purpose for our lives is invaluable! Other verses that show us He is our teacher and/or guide include Nehemiah 9:20; Ezekiel 36:27; Mark 13:11; Luke 12:12; and 1 Corinthians 2:10, 12–13.

In the beginning of the book of Acts, Paul writes that the resurrected Jesus told His disciples, "For John baptized with water, but you will be baptized with the Holy Spirit in a few days" (Acts 1:5).

As Jesus promised, the Holy Spirit came after Jesus was resurrected, and on the day of Pentecost, when the disciples were gathered in the upper room. The Holy Spirit empowered the early church to be witnesses "in Jerusalem, in all Judea and Samaria, and to the ends of the earth" (Acts 1:8).

Read Acts 2:1–4 and describe what happened when the Holy Spirit came.

Scripture describes the Holy Spirit as a dove (Luke 3:22), the finger of God (Luke 11:20), spiritual water (John 7:37–39), breath or wind (Acts 2:2), and the seal and promise of our salvation (Ephesians 1:13–14). Of all the ways the Bible refers to the Holy Spirit, I find most interesting that He is represented by the oil of the olive tree.

Zechariah, one of the Old Testament prophets, had a vision, and the meaning of the vision has several layers that I want us to dive into. Overall, included in the passage is a message to us regarding how we're to put our trust in the power of God's Holy Spirit working through us.

To begin working through the layers we want to study, read Zechariah 4:1–6 and 11–14.

> *The angel who was speaking with me then returned and roused me as one awakened out of sleep. He asked me, "What do you see?"*
>
> *I replied, "I see a solid gold lampstand with a bowl at the top. The lampstand also has seven lamps at the top with seven spouts for each of the lamps. There are also two olive trees beside it, one on the right of the bowl and the other on its left."*
>
> *Then I asked the angel who was speaking with me, "What are these, my lord?"*
>
> *"Don't you know what they are?" replied the angel who was speaking with me.*
>
> *I said, "No, my lord."*
>
> *So he answered me, "This is the word of the LORD to Zerubbabel: 'Not by strength or by might, but by my Spirit,' says the LORD of Armies."*
>
> *. . . I asked him, "What are the two olive trees on the right and left of the lampstand?" And I questioned him further, "What are the two streams of the olive trees, from which the golden oil is pouring through the two golden conduits?"*
>
> *Then he inquired of me, "Don't you know what these are?"*
>
> *"No, my lord," I replied.*
>
> *"These are the two anointed ones," he said, "who stand by the Lord of the whole earth."*
> ZECHARIAH 4:1–6, 11–14

Let's start with the historical context of this vision. In about 520 BC, the children of Israel were returning from seventy years of captivity in Babylon. Jerusalem's temple and city had been destroyed, and the people in the land opposed and fought the efforts to rebuild the temple. "After laying the foundation, God's people grew discouraged and for fourteen years, they took no further action . . . until God spoke through His prophets Haggai and Zechariah.[5]

This brings us to the passage we read. Zechariah sees a seven-armed, solid-gold lampstand with a bowl on top. One olive tree sits to its left and one to its right. Oil from the two trees funnels into the bowl. The bowl provides oil to the seven branches, which provide the light. Zechariah sees two streams of olive oil pouring through two golden conduits. The meaning of this vision becomes clear when we understand a couple of its key elements.

Olive Trees: Zechariah was informed that the two olive trees represented two individuals—Joshua the high priest and Zerubbabel the governor—who stood with the Lord (Zechariah 3–4; Revelation 11:3–4).

Oil: The lampstand can't burn without oil, so clearly the oil is essential. But this oil isn't ordinary oil. First, it comes from a bowl that is above the lampstand! And, second, it has a continuous flow from above. Zechariah 4:6 makes it clear what the oil is: "'Not by strength or by might, but by my Spirit,' says the LORD."

The oil represents the Spirit of God given without end. The vision pictures the people of God relying on the Spirit of God to fulfill the purposes of God. What a powerful example of how the Holy Spirit is our helper!

Take some time to reflect on Zechariah 4:6. Why do you think God gave this vision with this message when He did?

Think about the correlation between the oil, the Holy Spirit, and us. How might the continuous flow of oil to the lampstands relate to the Holy Spirit in our lives?

And don't get drunk with wine, which leads to reckless living, but be filled by the Spirit.
EPHESIANS 5:18

The fact that we are commanded to be filled shows that we have a responsibility to be filled. We are not just passive participants. When we are filled with the Spirit, we are making much of the great grace of His presence and help in our lives.

Read the following verses and write what they reveal about how we are filled and are to be led by the Holy Spirit.

ROMANS 8:1–17

GALATIANS 5:16–25

I love that the Holy Spirit is in us and with us always. He's ever-present to help us with every aspect of our lives. He's as real as our Heavenly Father and Jesus . . . and like the other two persons of the Trinity, He is someone to get to know and talk to.

PRAY

Leader (or volunteer) read the prayer aloud, or pray independently over your group before closing your time together.

Holy Spirit, I want to live filled with You. Please fill me fresh today and help me to have ears to hear You and a heart that is quick to respond to Your leading and conviction. As I go about my day, give me the wisdom, strength, and insight to know what to say and who to say it to, that more people may come to know Jesus and be filled with You. In Jesus' name, amen.

DAY 4 Liquid Gold

On one of my excursions to an olive farm a team was processing the recent harvest. They were operating a modern-day pressing machine, something I was eager to see. It was quite innovative, and yet, when the oil came out of the machine and filled the bottles, it was just as smooth and beautiful as the oil I'd seen pressed from using more traditional methods. And when I tasted it, I mentally started comparing it to the varietals grown on the farm and noting the ones I could detect.

The process of tasting olive oil is actually akin to tasting wine. First, you "sniff to identify the aromas", then you slurp to "emulsify the oil," spreading it through your mouth, and as you swallow, you "take note of which flavors you taste."[1]

Words used to describe what you taste in olive oil can include any number of things: artichoke, cinnamon, eucalyptus, grass, green almond, ripe apple, green banana, mint, pine, butter, flowers, nuts, black pepper, cherry, citrus, green tea, hay, or wood.[2] The taste is influenced by the varietal of olive and olive tree, the soil, sun, and water, the location on the planet, the conditions of each year of growth and harvest. That's right, like any crop, one year's harvest can taste better than another.

In the pages of Homer's *Iliad*, the work that the ancient Greek poet wrote around 762 BC, give or take fifty years, he referred to olive oil as "liquid gold."[3] When you see it come straight out of a press, Homer's description fits perfectly. And when you get to taste it with a discerning palate, you only want more.

The best olive oil to taste is what comes out of the press first because it's real virgin oil, and normally, it's a delicate light green. I understand that by the time olive oil reaches our local supermarkets, it can get confusing with all the different descriptions—cold pressed, virgin, extra virgin, and so on—but the best kind of oil to drink or pour on a salad is what is pressed out of the olives first, even after it's bottled and shipped to stores. If you just want something for cooking, then anything that's not virgin is sufficient.

Have you ever visited an olive farm and tasted olive oil right after it was pressed? Hopefully, you'll get the chance to, especially after walking through this study. There's something about seeing the olive trees, that produced the olives, that produced the oil, that seems to make it taste that much better to me.

All this talk about *seeing* and *tasting* brings to mind a verse from Psalm 34. David penned it during a difficult time in his life, yet it's in a series of psalms focused on giving thanks to God.

Read Psalm 34:8 and write it here.

We can understand how to taste and see that something like olive oil is good, but how do we taste and see that the Lord is good?

To begin gaining more understanding about this, let's look at all the verses in Psalm 34 in light of the context of David's life. The psalm opens with a reference to 1 Samuel 21. There David is on the run from King Saul, who is out to kill him. In a city called Nob, the priest Ahimelech has given David the sword of Goliath. From there, David flees to Gath where King Achish is in charge, and there he hears that people had begun to sing, "Saul has killed his thousands, but David his tens of thousands" (1 Samuel 21:11).

Afraid of what King Achish might do to him, David feigns insanity, scribbling on the city gate and letting saliva run down his beard (1 Samuel 21:12–13). His improvisation works. When King Achish sees him, he says, "Look! You can see the man is crazy. . . . Why did you bring him to me? Do I have such a shortage of crazy people that you brought this one to act crazy around me? Is this one going to come into my house?" (1 Samuel 21:14–15). From Gath, David continues to flee and takes refuge in the cave of Adullam (1 Samuel 22:1).

With all this in mind, let's read Psalm 34:1–8.

First, David praises God for delivering him from fear and trouble.

I will bless the LORD at all times; his praise will always be on my lips.
I will boast in the LORD; the humble will hear and be glad.
Proclaim the LORD's greatness with me; let us exalt his name together.
I sought the LORD, and he answered me and rescued me from all my fears.
Those who look to him are radiant with joy; their faces will never be ashamed.
This poor man cried, and the LORD heard him and saved him from all his troubles.
PSALM 34:1–6

Next, David calls upon the people of Israel to remember that their God is both their protector and deliverer.

> *The angel of the LORD encamps around those who fear him, and rescues them.*
> **PSALM 34:7**

And then, David encourages them (and us) to seek the Lord and know His goodness; that we will be blessed when we put our trust in the Lord.

> *Taste and see that the LORD is good. How happy is the person who takes refuge in him!*
> **PSALM 34:8**

I find it extraordinary that David starts the psalm with praise, then admonishment, and then encouragement to "taste and see that the LORD is good" with all he's going through. He experiences answers, deliverance, joy, salvation, rescues, angels, nearness, redemption, provision, protection, refuge, and more. And he did all this while simultaneously enduring great difficulty.

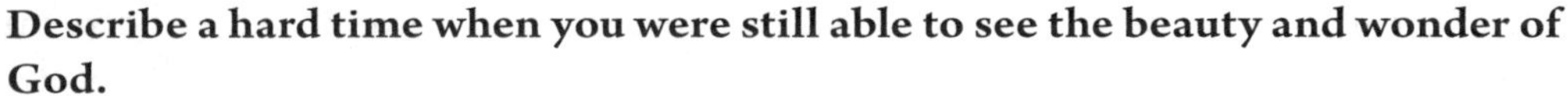

Describe a hard time when you were still able to see the beauty and wonder of God.

David's circumstances didn't get much better. I imagine we all have experienced times like that—when we've given God a sacrifice of praise in the midst of suffering and difficulty, when we've put our trust in Him and not much changed . . . at least not at first. In a good way, this psalm challenges me to remember to this. I especially noticed in this psalm that David experienced the goodness of God through *tangible* and *spiritual* experiences.

Tangible

Capable of being perceived especially by the sense of touch.[4]

Spiritual

[Gk. *pneumatikós, en pneúmati* (Rom. 2:29), *logikós* (Rom. 12:1; 1 Pet. 2:2)]. . . . It is used to designate that which is not, or is not only, physical or literal, but exists, or also exists, in the world of spirits, demons, angels, and God.[5]

Do you remember what your five physical senses are? List as many as you can remember.

1.

2.

3.

4.

5.

Did you remember that tasting and seeing are two of our God-given senses? Include them now if you didn't, and put a star by those two in your list.

For me, seeing a particular food naturally makes it more appealing to me. I want to see what I'm eating for it to look enticing. It's my sense of sight that helps me determine if I want to engage my sense of taste. For you, it might be your sense of smell that makes your mouth water and want to take a bite.

God's Word is full of references to seeing and sight. How many times does the Word tell us to look up or look to Jesus? Read Hebrews 12:1–2 and note what it tells us. (To *dig deeper*, you can also read Psalm 121:1–2.)

The Word is also full of references to food, hunger, and thirst for experiencing facets of God. Read the following verses and note how they might apply to the idea of tasting the goodness of God.

How sweet your word is to my taste—sweeter than honey in my mouth.
PSALM 119:103

> *Jesus said, "Everyone who drinks from this water will get thirsty again. But whoever drinks from the water that I will give him will never get thirsty again. In fact, the water I will give him will become a well of water springing up in him for eternal life."*
> JOHN 4:13–14

For me, hiking up a mountain, walking on a beach, or riding my bike along a trail reminds me of God's goodness. When I spend time laughing with Nick and my girls or talking into the wee hours of the night with friends, I experience facets of His goodness through their lives.

> **Identify a few ways you taste and see that the Lord is good in your life. Make your list here.**

Earlier this week we talked about Jesus calling Himself and us the light of the world. Today, I want to draw your attention to something else He called us; it's found in the verse that precedes where He said we are the light of the world, and it has to do with taste—in a spiritual sense.

> **Read Matthew 5:13 and fill in the blanks.**
>
> *"You are the ____________________ of the earth. But if the ____________________ loses its ____________________, how can it be made ____________________ again? It is no longer good for anything, except to be thrown out and trampled underfoot."*
> MATTHEW 5:13 NIV

When we cook and add salt, what does it do? It enhances food, doesn't it? It brings out the flavor. It also adds a vital nutrient to our diet. We can use salt to preserve raw meat. When we add it to foods we harvest from our gardens to can or freeze, we typically add salt as a preservative.

With all these ideas in mind, write why you think God called us the salt of the earth.

If salt affects everything it comes in contact with, how might we affect all the people we interact with? Colossians 4:6 tells us, "Let your speech always be gracious, seasoned with salt, so that you may know how you should answer each person."

As we taste and see that the Lord is good, we live as salt and light in this world, helping others taste and see that the Lord is good.

PRAY

Leader (or volunteer) read the prayer aloud, or pray independently over your group before closing your time together.

My prayer for you today is based on Psalm 34:8: "Taste and see that the Lord is good."

Heavenly Father, in all our busyness and doing, help us to remember to taste and see that You are good, and then to help others taste and see that You are good, too. Help us to be salt and light in a world that is starving for a taste of You. Help us to bring people to the source of true life—You and You alone. In Jesus' name, amen.

DAY 5 Guided Prayer and Journaling

> *But I am like a flourishing olive tree in the house of God;*
> *I trust in God's faithful love forever and ever.*
>
> PSALM 52:8

There's a story in 1 Kings that goes so well with all that we've studied about olive oil this week, particularly how the oil of the Holy Spirit never runs out for us. It's a short narrative from the life of Elijah, telling of the time when God sent him to the widow of Zarephath. The region was experiencing a great famine, yet God sent Elijah to meet the widow so she could feed him (1 Kings 17). When Elijah arrived at the city gate, she was there, gathering wood for a fire so she could cook one last meal for her son and herself.

Despite how desperate it all was, Elijah did as God instructed him and he said to her,

> *"Please bring me a little water in a cup and let me drink." As she went to get it, he called to her and said, "Please bring me a piece of bread in your hand."*
>
> *But she said, "As the Lord your God lives, I don't have anything baked—only a handful of flour in the jar and a bit of oil in the jug. Just now, I am gathering a couple of sticks in order to go prepare it for myself and my son so we can eat it and die."*
>
> *Then Elijah said to her, "Don't be afraid; go and do as you have said. But first make me a small loaf from it and bring it out to me. Afterward, you may make some for yourself and your son, for this is what the Lord God of Israel says, 'The flour jar will not become empty and the oil jug will not run dry until the day the Lord sends rain on the surface of the land.'"*
>
> 1 KINGS 17:10-16

So she proceeded to do according to the word of Elijah. Then the woman, Elijah, and her household ate for many days. The flour jar did not become empty, and the oil jug did not run dry, according to the word of the Lord he had spoken through Elijah.

Just like the two lampstands from Zechariah 4, this woman's flour jar and oil were supernaturally and continuously replenished. She never ran out.

As we close out our week with prayer and journaling, I want us to think about how the oil of the Holy Spirit never runs out—His presence, help, guidance, influence, direction, answers, strength, and insight. Like the oil of the olive trees continuously flowing into the lampstands, He never runs out.

I don't so much want you to ask Him for anything in today's time of reflection, but I'd rather you focus on what He offers us . . . and how there are no limits to what He can give us . . . and there are no interruptions in the supply chain.

Do you need answers?

Do you need healing?

Do you need direction?

Do you need peace?

Do you need joy?

Do you need hope?

Do you need to feel God's love?

Do you need strengthening?

Do you need help changing?

Do you need to know what to do next?

The Holy Spirit is ever-ready and ever-present to help you. It was Jesus who said:

> *"If you love me, you will keep my commands. And I will ask the Father, and he will give you another Counselor to be with you forever. He is the Spirit of truth. The world is unable to receive him because it doesn't see him or know him. But you do know him, because he remains with you and will be in you."*
> **JOHN 14:15–17**

You don't have to do anything alone. You don't have to go it alone. You don't have to figure it out all by yourself. And you weren't intended to! You have the Holy Spirit within you to help you.

WEEK 5

Growing in Health

GROUP STUDY

Watch

Watch the video for Week 5: Growing in Health, recording your thoughts as you listen.

"God wants you to be happy."

> *Happy is the one who does not walk in the advice of the wicked. . . . Instead, his delight is in the Lord's instruction. . . . He is like a tree planted beside flowing streams that bears its fruit in its season, and its leaf does not wither. Whatever he does prospers.*
> PSALM 1:1–3

God's intent for us is not merely to survive but to thrive. Many of us, however, find ourselves in a state of "languishing."

> *Guard your heart above all else, for it is the source of life.*
> PROVERBS 4:23

An unguarded heart is vulnerable to bitterness, anxiety, and impurities that prevent flourishing. Guarding it is an active, ongoing process.

> *Be transformed by the renewing of your mind.*
> ROMANS 12:2

We must intentionally replace worldly or negative thought patterns with God's truth.

> *Your body is a temple of the Holy Spirit. . . . So glorify God with your body.*
> 1 CORINTHIANS 6:19–20

True happiness is found in delighting in God, leading to a flourishing life. We must actively move from languishing to flourishing by tending to our spiritual health.

Holistic health is essential: We must intentionally care for our hearts, minds, and bodies as interconnected parts of a whole.

> *But I am like a flourishing olive tree in the house of God; I trust in God's faithful love forever and ever.*
> PSALM 52:8

Discuss

Leader (or volunteer), read the following aloud to the group and follow with the prompts for discussion.

The session opened with the statement: "God wants you to be happy."

What was your initial, honest reaction to hearing this? Does it align with or challenge what you have previously been taught about the Christian life?

Psalm 1:1–3 connects true happiness (or being "blessed") to delighting in God's instruction.

> *How happy is the one who does not walk in the advice of the wicked or stand in the pathway with sinners or sit in the company of mockers! Instead, his delight is in the Lord's instruction, and he meditates on it day and night. He is like a tree planted beside flowing streams that bears its fruit in its season, and its leaf does not wither. Whatever he does prospers.*
>
> PSALM 1:1–3

How does this biblical definition of happiness differ from the world's pursuit of happiness?

The concept of "languishing" was also introduced. In what season of your life have you most identified with this feeling of languishing?

Jeremiah 31:25 reads: "For I will satisfy the weary soul, and every languishing soul I will replenish" (ESV). What does this promise mean to you personally?

Spiritual flourishing requires a holistic approach to health: heart, mind, and body.

Heart Health: **Proverbs 4:23 says, "Guard your heart above all else, for it is the source of life."**

What are some practical ways you "guard" your heart against influences that can hinder your spiritual well-being?

Mental Health: **Romans 12:2 calls us to "be transformed by the renewing of your mind."**

What is one negative or anxious thought pattern God is helping you to replace with His truth right now?

Physical Health: **1 Corinthians 6:19–20 describes our bodies as temples of the Holy Spirit.**

How does viewing your body as something to be stewarded for God's glory change your perspective on physical health and self-care?

Reflect on the deep connection between these three areas. Can you share an example from your own life where neglecting one area (heart, mind, or body) negatively impacted the others? Conversely, how have you seen intentional care in one area produce positive effects across the board?

Our challenge for this week is to conduct a personal health assessment. Of the three areas discussed—heart, mind, and body—which one requires the most intentional focus for you in this current season? How can this group specifically pray for and encourage you as you seek to cultivate health in that area?

GROW

Consider these responses to what you've seen and heard today.

- Think of one idea you can take toward your own happiness and do it.
- Think of one person you can encourage, cheer up, and bring happiness to this week, and then make a plan to do it! Write their name here and what you plan to do for or with them.

PRAY

Leader (or volunteer) read the prayer aloud, or pray independently over your group before closing your time together.

My prayer for you is based on Proverbs 28:14, "Happy is the one who is always reverent."

Heavenly Father, help me to fully grasp how You want me to be happy, and help me actually be happy. I give You all the reverence I know how to give by taking You seriously, respecting You deeply, and honoring You greatly. Help me live my life looking to You as my ultimate authority. Thank You for helping me flourish like a healthy green olive tree. In Jesus' name I pray, amen.

WEEK 5 | Growing in Health

PERSONAL STUDY

The steady rhythm of daily devotion is a vital part of flourishing in your life with Jesus. Set aside time this week to really dig into God's Word. Each day, open yourself up to the Spirit's work in your heart and mind. Then, prayerfully reflect on the beautiful truth He is revealing during this season of new growth.

DAY 1
Our Spiritual Health

DAY 2
Our Heart Health

DAY 3
A Healthy Mind

DAY 4
A Healthy Body

DAY 5
Guided Prayer and Journaling

DAY 1 Our Spiritual Health

Olive trees are known for surviving adverse conditions. Like we mentioned in the first week of our study, because of their hardy root system, even if something devastating happens to the trunk and foliage aboveground, it's possible for the root system belowground to revive the tree. It's this kind of resilience that explains why there are olive trees on the planet that are thousands of years old. In fact, the oldest olive trees in existence have withstood natural disasters of all kinds— including forest fires—and they've withstood the rise of civilization and all that comes with people populating the world around them. You can see the most ancient of them all in Greece, Lebanon, and Israel.[1]

Two of the oldest are on the island of Crete. One is referred to as the olive tree of Vouves and it's confirmed to be two thousand years old based on tree ring analysis, though some say it's between three thousand and four thousand years old.[2] And it still produces olives! I can't help but think of that verse that speaks of the righteous saying, "They will still bear fruit in old age, healthy and green" (Psalm 92:14–15). I do want to be like an olive tree that produces fruit well into my older years. I want to keep flourishing, don't you?

The other ancient olive tree on Crete is called Azores, and the diameter of its trunk is a little over twenty-three feet. The circumference of its crown is more than one hundred thirteen feet.[3] Can you imagine?

In northern Lebanon, there is a cluster of sixteen ancient trees affectionately referred to as the "sisters." They are thought to be six thousand years old, and they too still produce olives.[4]

In the Bethlehem district of Israel, there are trees believed to be three thousand and four thousand years old.[5]

The resiliency of olive trees is astounding, and yet, despite all this enduring vitality, like all living things, it is possible for olive trees to grow sick, to begin to languish, and need attention if they are to continue flourishing.

When an olive tree grows sick, there are often telltale signs that give clear indications of what's causing the sickness. They can begin to have yellow or brown dry and brittle leaves. They can have spotted or wilted leaves and drop them earlier than they should in a normal year of growth.[6] They can begin to have branches that snap easily. Their trunks can become mushy and cracked, particularly if they are dying. If an olive tree has a fungal disease, there can be a discoloring at its base. Olive trees can become infected with pests or develop conditions like fruit mummification.[7]

I could keep going, but my point is this: David said, "But I am like a flourishing olive tree in the house of God; I trust in God's faithful love forever" (Psalm 52:8). We are like olive trees, and even olive trees, whose numerous cultivars are some of the most hardy and resilient trees in the world, sometimes begin to languish. In other words, there are seasons in our spiritual lives where we're spiritually healthy and thriving, and there are times when, perhaps because of enduring seasons of being busy, productive, and fruitful—or perhaps from enduring seasons of having one thing after another happening to us—we begin to grow weary. We begin to grow tired. And we need to be replenished so we can keep running our race. None of us, no matter how long we've walked with Jesus, are impervious to the need of regularly tending to our spiritual health.

Do you regularly tend to your spiritual health? Or do you wait until you're tired or burned out to replenish? Write your thoughts here.

We want to be like olive trees who are whole, healthy, and flourishing, but without care, we could become like olive trees who are languishing. In a psalm of lament, David wrote, "Be gracious to me, O LORD, for I am languishing; heal me, O LORD, for my bones are troubled" (Psalm 6:2 ESV).

Flourishing is "marked by vigorous and healthy growth."[8] Languishing, on the other hand, is "the antithesis of flourishing."[9]

Languishing

Languishing means "to be or become feeble, weak, or enervated." It can be defined as listlessness, as living "in a state of . . . decreasing vitality." It can be an inability to move forward, to be "dispirited," or "to suffer neglect." Think of its use in these sentences:

"Plants *languish* in the drought."
He "*languished* in prison for ten years."
"The bill *languished* in the Senate for eight months."[10]

Languishing can also be described as "apathy, a sense of restlessness or feeling unsettled or an overall lack of interest in life or the things that typically bring you joy." It can be a "series of emotions"; it can "encompass . . . distressing feelings of stagnation, monotony, and emptiness."[11] It can be when you feel "indifferent to your indifference."[12]

How would you rate your spiritual health with 1 being languishing and 10 being flourishing?

1	2	3	4	5	6	7	8	9	10
languishing									*flourishing*

If you rated your spiritual health on the lower end of the continuum, God understands where you are and He wants to replenish you. "For I will [fully] satisfy the weary soul, and I will replenish every languishing and sorrowful person" (Jeremiah 31:25 AMPC).

Wherever we are on the continuum, God wants to replenish us. He wants to help us be green, flourishing olive trees, and He understands the times we're not.

For example, when an olive tree is leggy, it means the tree "appears to have stretched out branches and stems, with sparse or spread-out leaves. . . . [and its] branches and stems are becoming weaker and thin."[13] I can't help but think of how we often say we're "stretched thin" when we get too much on our plates and are juggling all the things. Maybe we should start saying we're "leggy" instead. For a short person like me, that sounds much more appealing!

Even Jesus needed to be replenished and to give His spiritual health attention. The following verses show us what Jesus did.

Matthew 11:19 | *Ate and drank*

Mark 1:35; 6:46 | *Rose early and prayed*

Mark 6:30–32 | *Stopped to rest*

Luke 22:7–8 | *Made plans for dinner and celebrated Passover with His friends*

John 13:23 | *Spent time with those He loved, His friends*

If you're languishing, perhaps it's time to practice some of Jesus' responses—both His physical soul care strategies and His spiritual practices.

Consider the following list of soul care ideas. Put a star by the ones that refresh you.

SLEEPING	TRAVELING	BEING WITH FRIENDS
EATING	CLEANING	GOING ON A DATE
WALKING	ORGANIZING	WORKING OUT
READING	DECORATING	PLAYING WITH YOUR KIDS
VOLUNTEERING	DIY PROJECTS	VISITING A MUSEUM
BIKING	CRAFTING	PLANTING FLOWERS
DINING OUT	HIKING	NEEDLEWORK
LAUGHING	SHOPPING	SPORTS

We need to care for ourselves physically and spiritually. Our spiritual health stems from a healthy relationship with God. Consider the list below for how you can cultivate your connection with God. Check off the ones you frequently engage in.

PERSONAL PRAYER	JOURNALING	GATHERING WITH OTHER CHRISTIANS
TIMES OF SILENCE	READING CHRISTIAN BOOKS	ATTENDING CHURCH
FASTING	SERVING OTHERS	BIBLE STUDY
READING YOUR BIBLE	GENEROSITY	DISCIPLESHIP
MEMORIZING BIBLE VERSES	PRAYER WITH OTHER CHRISTIANS	FELLOWSHIP/ FRIENDSHIP
WORSHIP	REST/SABBATH	EXPERIENCING CREATION

We can connect with God and move forward in our spiritual formation in so many ways—through podcasts, devotionals, Bible apps, and online studies. We're not always in seasons where we can spend lengthy periods of time on any particular part of our lives, but with every step we take toward God, we are more likely to find ourselves flourishing rather than languishing.

What changes can you make in your life to incorporate at least one of the practices you have identified this week? It's completely understandable if you need to modify another practice to make room for a new one.

PRAY

Leader (or volunteer) read the prayer aloud, or pray independently over your group before closing your time together.

As we close out our day, my prayer for you is based on 2 Peter 3:18: "Grow in the grace and knowledge of our Lord and Savior Jesus Christ."

Heavenly Father, please keep us growing so we have a healthy spiritual life. Show us the most effective spiritual practices for the season of life we're in to keep flourishing. Thank You that as we keep taking steps toward You, we flourish like olive trees in the house of God, trusting in Your faithful love forever and ever. In Jesus' name, amen.

DAY 2 Our Heart Health

"Alright, Mrs. Caine, you're good for another year," my doctor said, "I won't see you until then, unless, of course, you decide to fracture something else on one of your hiking adventures. Do your best to stay safe out there, okay?"

Laughing with my doctor who never missed a chance to tease me about my hiking injuries, I promised to take care of myself on the trail as well as off the trail. We had just gone over all my test results from my annual physical and I was good to go. I so appreciated how thorough she was, always checking me out from head to toe and listening to any new symptoms that concerned me.

Of all the many pokes and prods and tests, she always ensures my heart is thoroughly examined. I've never had any heart issues, nonetheless, monitoring my heart health is essential. Somewhere in the course of evaluating my heart, she requires I get an electrocardiogram and an echocardiogram.

The electrocardiogram (EKG) is the test where the technician attaches little electrodes to my chest and I get on a treadmill and run uphill—and while I do, the technician monitors my heart and a machine records the rhythmic beats.

The echocardiogram is where a technician takes an ultrasound of my heart to examine the chambers and to monitor how the blood is flowing in and out of each one.

The results of these tests, along with the bloodwork that checks my cholesterol and triglyceride levels, lets my doctor know if all is well and flourishing, or if something needs further attention. When I meet with her to discuss the results of all the tests, she never fails to remind me to keep exercising and eating healthy foods, so I maintain optimal heart health.

In my spiritual journey, I have found that our spiritual hearts need the same kind of checkups and care. Read Proverbs 4:23 and fill in the blanks.

__________________ *your* __________________ *above all else,*

for it is the __________________ *of* __________________ .

PROVERBS 4:23

How would you describe what it means to guard your heart?

Both literally and spiritually, our hearts are the source of life. On the next page, consider the 360-degree view of our heart . . .

The Heart

[The heart is the] center of the physical, mental, and spiritual life of humans. The word "heart" refers to the physical organ and is considered to be the center of the physical life. Eating and drinking are spoken of as strengthening the heart (Gen. 18:5; Judg. 19:5; Acts 14:17). As the center of physical life, the heart came to stand for the person as a whole. It became the focus for all the vital functions of the body, including both intellectual and spiritual life.

The heart and the intellect are closely connected, the heart being the seat of intelligence: "For this people's heart has grown callous . . . otherwise they might . . . understand with their hearts and turn back" (Matt. 13:15 HCSB).

The heart is connected with thinking: As a person "thinketh in his heart, so is he" (Prov. 23:7 KJV). To ponder something in one's heart means to consider it carefully (Luke 1:66; 2:19). "To set one's heart on" is the literal Hebrew that means to give attention to something, or even to worry about it (1 Sam. 9:20). To call to heart (mind) something means to remember something (Isa. 46:8). All of these are functions of the mind but are connected with the heart in biblical language.[1]

Our hearts are the epicenter of our internal lives. Think of how we communicate this: "following our hearts," "having a change of heart," or "losing heart." For example, if someone loses motivation in their career or affection in a relationship, they might say "my heart is no longer in it."

Describe an area of your life where you've "lost heart" and your "heart is no longer in it."

A loss of heart is not always a bad thing. A loss of heart in one area can be driven by a growing love of the heart in another area, like replacing love for the world with love for God.

That said, a loss of heart for God and the things of God is dangerous. Our spiritual hearts can malfunction with weakness, brokenness, or pain, particularly when we've faced rejection, humiliation, betrayal, abandonment, addiction, loss, grief, and more. Such wounds can often lead to doubt, fear, bitterness, disappointment, rage, jealousy, defeat, and hopelessness.

Wounds inflicted on our hearts affect us mentally, emotionally, and spiritually. And because they don't bleed externally, like a cut everyone can see, it can seem like no one notices.

Write what painful wound(s) come to mind as you read this.

Read the promises in Psalm 147:3 and Psalm 34:18 and fill in the blanks below.

He heals the ____________________ *and* ____________________ *their wounds.*

PSALM 147:3

The L*ORD is near the* ____________________*; he saves those* ____________________ *in spirit.*

PSALM 34:18

How does the truth of these verses give you strength today for the wound(s) you listed?

As we discover God's healing for our hearts, we continue the journey toward spiritual health. So, let's prayerfully evaluate the state of our hearts using two heart diagnostics Jesus gave us: our treasure and our words.

First, Jesus said, "Where your treasure is your heart will be also" (Matthew 6:21). Notice He does not say, "Where your heart is your treasure will be." Instead, Jesus is making it clear that our investments direct our hearts more than our hearts direct our investments.

Where do you invest the best and the most of your time, talent, and treasure?

Are those investments directing your heart toward health, toward a greater love for God and the things of God?

Second, Jesus gave a second diagnostic: "For the mouth speaks from the overflow of the heart" (Matthew 12:34). Our words show the condition of our hearts.

Ask God to help you recall and accurately reflect upon the words you spoke this week. Use five words to summarize the qualities and characteristics of those words.

As you look at that list, consider how you can pray for greater heart health. What needs to be uprooted from your heart? What needs to fill it? Ask God to uproot and fill . . . and show you specific steps you can take to grow in guarding the source of your life.

PRAY

Leader (or volunteer) read the prayer aloud, or pray independently over your group before closing your time together.

Knowing that we're to be flourishing like an olive tree in the house of God, trusting in His faithful love forever and ever—and with our hearts in mind—my prayer for you today is based on Job 14:7: "There is hope for a tree: If it is cut down, it will sprout again, and its shoots will not die."

Heavenly Father, I ask You to help us sprout again, to grow, thrive, and flourish. Help us to come alive and move forward, ever fulfilling all Your plans and purpose for our lives. Help us to walk in Your joy. In Jesus' name we pray, amen.

DAY 3 A Healthy Mind

I'm always thinking about something. I have the kind of mind where my wheels are turning before I even open my eyes in the morning, and they don't stop until after my eyes are closed at night and I've drifted off to sleep. Even then, I'm not sure my wheels ever stop turning completely; I just don't remember what I'm thinking when I think in my sleep . . . I think.

To be honest, I love to think. I love thinking about thinking. But I also have the tendency to overthink. Shocking, I know. What's more, I've found that if I'm not careful, my thoughts can get the best of me, meaning they can start taking me places I don't really want to go—places that aren't good for me, places of worrying or ruminating over a conversation or imagining what might happen . . . instead of thinking about what is happening . . . or about all the good God is doing. Why is it that it's often easier to think about what isn't good than it is to think about what is good? For me, of all the areas of flourishing in my life, my greatest challenge has always been winning the battle that goes on in my mind.

I am so glad we are diving deep into studying how to have a healthy mind today; because the truths we are going to unpack have literally been a life saver for me. I once heard someone say, "Jesus saved my soul, but the Word of God changed my mind," and that is certainly true for me. Because of the trauma and pain of my past, I developed so many wrong thinking patterns early in life that I did not know were wrong. I mean we only know what we know right? And in my journey, I discovered that until we start thinking about what we're thinking about, we often don't even know we have patterns of thinking that aren't good, nor how they were developed.

So many of the obstacles I have had to overcome, in order to do what God has called me to do, were the battles I fought in my mind and for my mind—and not whatever obstacles I was encountering in my external world. It seems that every time I managed to change what was going on in my mind, I was much better equipped to overcome and do whatever God wanted me to do next—including overcoming the obstacles I faced.

In other words, to do all that God has called me to do, to become all that God made me to be, I've had to learn to replace my thoughts with God's thoughts—something vital to us all in our pursuit of flourishing as an olive tree in the house of God.

What are you thinking right now? You can write in code if you want—because it's probably good that we can't read each other's minds!

Whether you're thinking peaceful thoughts, or your mind is racing with worst-case scenarios, the good news is we can actually change our thoughts. In Mark 1:14–15, Jesus tells us to repent and believe the good news. The Greek word for *repent* is *metanoeó*, which means "think differently after."[1] We are called to repent of our sinful patterns, including our sinful, wrong patterns of thinking.

Read Romans 12:2 and fill in the blanks.

Do not be ____________________ *to this age, but be* ____________________
by the ____________________ *of your* ____________________, *so that you may*
____________________ *what is the* ____________________, ____________________,
and ____________________ *will of God.*

ROMANS 12:2

Renewing indicates major change—"to become new again . . . to take on fresh life."[2] Based on this, it's as though we can reprogram our minds, regardless of the patterns of thinking we have developed.

Read 1 Corinthians 2:16 to discover how this is possible. Write what you find.

If we have been given the mind of Christ, why don't we as Christians automatically think the thoughts of Christ? The best answer, like usual, is found in the Word.

Read Philippians 2:5–11 and record your insights. (Consider reading it in the NKJV for the most clarity.)

A few things about the first phrase in verse 5 really stand out to me. First, in the Greek, "let this mind be" is just one verb and it is an imperative (or command). This tells us that there is a role and responsibility we have in having the mind of Christ. Second, "let this mind be" is the Greek verb *phroneó*, meaning "regulate (moderate) from within, as inner-perspective (insight) shows itself in corresponding, outward behavior."[3] The mind of Christ starts with the perspective of Christ—seeing through His lens, seeing how and what He sees, and then responding His way. To have this perspective, we must create our own mindsets. A *mindset* is a "a mental inclination, tendency, or habit."[4]

Read Colossians 3:1–3 fill in the blanks.

If then you have been raised with Christ, seek the things that are above, where Christ is, seated at the right hand of God. ________ ______________ __________________ *on things that are above, not on things that are on earth. For you have died, and your life is hidden with Christ in God.*

COLOSSIANS 3:1–3 ESV

How might you set your mind each day? Write your ideas here.

Paul told us that we can choose what to think about (Colossians 3:1–3), and he told us what to think about (Phillipians 4:7–8). We're to think about what's true, honorable, just, pure, lovely, commendable, excellent, and worthy of praise.

- To think on something true is to think on what is "consistent with fact or reality,"[5] what's certain, reliable, and founded in the truth of the Word of God.
- To think on something honorable is to think on what is "noble," "dignified," and "worthy of respect"—including God, others, and ourselves.[6]
- To think on something just is to think on what is in conformity with justice, law, or morality; on what is honest, accurate and righteous.
- To think on something pure is to think on what is morally pure, innocent, and holy.
- To think on something lovely is to think on what is good, merry, pleasant, desirable, in order, usable, kind, and morally good.
- To think on something commendable is to think on what is well-spoken of, reputable, and of good report.
- To think on something excellent is to think on what is good and has excellence in character.
- To think on something worthy of praise is to think what is worthy of high commendation and of being thankful.[7]

Imagine what your life would become if you changed one thought a day to align with what God thinks and says? Write down one thought you've had today that needs to be changed (renewed). Then cross it out and write a replacement thought from the Word of God next to it.

Renewing our minds is not a once-and-done moment, but a daily process. Read 2 Corinthians 10:3–5 here and underline how we fight.

> *For although we live in the flesh, we do not wage war according to the flesh, since the weapons of our warfare are not of the flesh, but are powerful through God for the demolition of strongholds. We demolish arguments and every proud thing that is raised up against the knowledge of God, and we take every thought captive to obey Christ.*
> 2 CORINTHIANS 10:3–5

Notice that word *stronghold.*

Stronghold

The word "stronghold appears at least 50 times in the Bible. It commonly refer[s] to a fortress with a difficult access (see Judges 6:2; 1 Sam. 23:14)."[8]

In Jeremiah 16:19, the prophet uses the term in reference to God: "LORD, my strength and my stronghold, my refuge in a time of distress. . . ."

The Hebrew word for *stronghold* in these instances is *mauzzi* and it implies a structure, much like the city of Jerusalem.[9]

No wonder Paul used the word *stronghold* to refer to our minds and what runs through them. For me, strongholds have been thoughts that seemed to be a fortress, the ones on a never-ending circuit in my brain. These thoughts became *patterns of thinking* that I had to disrupt and replace. My past and shame would scream one thing, but I had to disrupt that internal voice with God's truth, even speaking it aloud to myself.

STRONGHOLD	SCRIPTURE
You are useless.	I am God's workmanship, created in Christ for good works (Ephesians 2:10).
You're not good enough.	I am the righteousness of God in Christ Jesus (2 Corinthians 5:21).
No one will ever love you.	I am greatly loved by God (Romans 1:7; Ephesians 2:4; Colossians 3:12).

Identify your own strongholds (recurring patterns of thinking) and scriptures that can combat them.

STRONGHOLD	SCRIPTURE

"Let this mind be in you" (Philippians 2:5 KJV) by submitting to the Spirit of God instead of striving against the Spirit of God as we set our minds on the truth of God.

PRAY

Leader (or volunteer) read the prayer aloud, or pray independently over your group before closing your time together.

As we close out our day, I pray that you would be empowered to take responsibility for your own mind and thoughts. The enemy can introduce thoughts, of course, but he can't make you run with any of them. Romans 8:5–6 tells us: "For those who live according to the flesh set their minds on the things of the flesh, but those who live according to the Spirit set their minds on the things of the Spirit. For to set the mind on the flesh is death, but to set the mind on the Spirit is life and peace" (ESV).

Heavenly Father, we live according to the Holy Spirit, so we set our minds on the things of the Spirit. We set our minds on things above, on what is true, honorable, just, pure, lovely, commendable, excellent, and worthy of praise. Thank You for giving us life and peace as we do. Thank You for helping us be like healthy flourishing olive trees. In Jesus' name, amen.

DAY 4 A Healthy Body

Since learning to hike a few years ago, I have hiked all kinds of terrain—and I have learned to love them all for the beauty and the adventure each of them has given me. To be honest, it amazes me that I can hike like I do, though I've always done my best to stay fit and take care of my body. I can remember doing aerobics in the eighties, before running and biking became such a passion for me, and then learning in my late forties how to lift weights and kickbox. But never would I have dreamed that I could hike up mountains and go such long distances like I do now. I'm so grateful God gave me friends who have taught me the skills necessary for enjoying it, and for a body that can still do it.

I remember one hike that wasn't supposed to be especially difficult. My friend Stephanie and I set out to hike Mt. Diablo, in Danville, California. It had rained the day before, but it never occurred to us that might be a problem.

At first the trail was what we expected—dry and easy, much like the beginnings of most trails—but when we began to hit the really steep sections, I was shocked to find stretches of mud. It wasn't dried out at all, and though I did my best to keep myself from sliding and moving forward, at one point I had to practically crawl on my hands and knees to pull myself up the mountain.

I even sank up to my knees and got stuck in the mud. No matter how hard I tried, I literally couldn't get my hiking boot to come up and out of the mud. When I tried to lift it, I almost came out of it. I did my best to curl my toes and try to grip the inside of my boot, but it was no use. Next, I grabbed the top edges of my boot and tried to raise my foot while tugging on my boot, but all that did was make me start to tip over and get mud all over my sleeves. No matter what I tried, it was no use, and all I could do was laugh.

Stephanie came to my rescue and, bracing herself, she began to pull me out. As I exited the muddy bog, I kept crawling as there was no other way to keep moving up the trail. When I finally reached a place where I could stand, I did, and my boots were covered in mud, as were my pants. Even my rain jacket was a muddy mess—front, back, sleeves and all.

By the time our hike was over, I had some new bruises and felt some aches and pains from working so hard getting through the mud, but I'm so glad I had the strength to manage it. All the weight training I'd done the past few years proved to be worth it in those moments. At my age and stage of life, I am so grateful every day that I have a body that can still do most of the things I love to do, including hiking. I know that's not everyone's story, and I never take it for granted.

In light of this, I want us to spend some time today focusing on the importance of looking after our bodies, to the best of our abilities and within our individual limitations, as a component of leading a flourishing life. After many years of studying the Word, I have discovered that God has a lot to say about our physical bodies, which indicates how much He cares about our bodies. Nothing we will study is designed to put shame or condemnation on anyone, but to inspire us all to want to pursue health—so we can flourish and do all that God has called us to do, because He's called us all to do something. He has plans and purpose for each and every one of us.

When God created us, our bodies were not an afterthought, but the actual vehicle God created for us to outwork His plans and purposes. Though our bodies are decaying day by day (2 Corinthians 4:16–18), they are a physical masterpiece. Our teeth are as strong as shark's teeth,[1] and our bodies glow (just too faintly for the human eye to detect).[2] An infant has three hundred bones that fuse with growth so that an adult has two hundred six,[3] and more than half of these bones are in our hands, wrists, feet, and ankles.[4] Our mouths produce 1.75 pints of saliva a day,[5] and our bodies produce twenty-five million new cells every moment.[6] With organs we have in pairs, we only need one to survive.[7] Sixty percent of our bodies are water,[8] and we have one hundred thousand miles of blood vessels in our bodies, enough to circle the equator four times![9] Information travels to our brain at 268 miles per hour,[10] our hearts beat one hundred thousand times a day,[11] and "scientists estimate that [our noses] can recognize a trillion different scents."[12]

Our bodies are a miracle! God made them a marvel of engineering because Ephesians 2:10 tells us we are His handiwork. We should be doing all we can to take care of our bodies. God wants every part of us to flourish—our spirits, souls, *and* bodies.

Read the following verses and underline the phrases that describe how God first made our physical bodies. (You can *dig deeper* by reading Genesis 1:27; Psalm 139:14; and John 1:14.)

In Genesis 2:7, God made Adam: "Then the LORD God formed the man out of the dust from the ground and breathed the breath of life into his nostrils, and the man became a living being."

Then, in Genesis 2:21–22, God made Eve: "So the LORD God caused a deep sleep to come over the man, and he slept. God took one of his ribs and closed the flesh at that place. Then the LORD God made the rib he had taken from the man into a woman and brought her to the man."

God designed, created, and gave us our physical bodies, but they actually *still belong to Him*, especially for those in Christ.

Read the following verse and answer the questions that follow.

> *Don't you know that your body is a temple of the Holy Spirit who is in you, whom you have from God? You are not your own, for you were bought at a price. So glorify God with your body.*
> 1 CORINTHIANS 6:19–20

Who lives in your body?

Who does God say owns your body?

What are we to do with our bodies?

What were our bodies bought with?

In the Old Testament, the temple was a sacred meeting place for the Israelites, the habitation of God, where He revealed His glory and gave instructions (Exodus 25:8; 1 Kings 6).[13] With Jesus' resurrection, the New Testament speaks of the temple of God as both the gathering of believers (Ephesians 2:19–22) and as our bodies.

Our hyper-sexualized, image-based, self-gratifying, pleasure-driven world encourages and celebrates whatever we want to do with our bodies. But when we realize that Jesus bought us with His own blood (1 Peter 1:18–19), and that He owns us—spirit, soul, and body—it changes how we see, fuel, and steward our bodies here on earth, doesn't it? Surrendering our bodies to the Lordship of Jesus is not easy, but it leads to life.

For we know that if our earthly tent we live in is destroyed, we have a building from God, an eternal dwelling in the heavens, not made with hands.
2 CORINTHIANS 5:1

All throughout Scripture, we see God call upon us to steward what He loans us and entrusts to our care. This stewardship includes our body.

Read the following verses and, using two different colors, highlight:
1) What God considers to be a healthy way to steward our bodies; and
2) What God considers to be some unhealthy ways to use our bodies.

"Everything is permissible for me," but not everything is beneficial.

"Everything is permissible for me," but I will not be mastered by anything.

"Food is for the stomach and the stomach for food," and God will do away with both of them. However, the body is not for sexual immorality but for the Lord, and the Lord for the body.

God raised up the Lord and will also raise us up by his power.

Don't you know that your bodies are a part of Christ's body?
1 CORINTHIANS 6:12–15

We live in a world where there are countless ways to misuse our bodies: from overeating, overworking, to abusing alcohol or substances, and lacking exercise, rest, and sleep. So much is *permissible*, but not *beneficial*. In order to flourish in life, it makes sense to do the things that are beneficial and to cease doing those things that are not.

Permissible vs. Beneficial

In the Greek, *permissible* means "to be allowed, especially as according to rule or custom."[14]
Beneficial means to be "advantageous."[15]

Let's dig a little deeper. Look up the following verses and summarize what each verse says we are to do—or not do—with our bodies.

SCRIPTURE	ACTIONS
EXODUS 34:21	
MARK 12:20–31; EPHESIANS 5:28–29	
ROMANS 6:13	
1 CORINTHIANS 9:27	

Are you making the most of what God has given you? Earlier today we read 1 Corinthians 6:20 which told us to "glorify God with your body."

Glorify and Glory

The word *glorify* in 1 Corinthians 6:20 means "positively acknowledging, recognizing, or esteeming someone's character, nature, or attributes."[16] In the Greek, it is *dŏxazō,* meaning "to render (or esteem) glorious (in a wide application):—(make) glorify(-ious), full of (have) glory, honour, and magnify."[17]

Later in 1 Corinthians 10:31, Paul uses another form of the word *glorify*; he uses *glory*. In the Greek, it's *doxa,* meaning "glory (as very apparent), in a wide application . . . dignity, glory (-ious), honor, praise, worship."[18]

So, whether you eat or drink, or whatever you do, do everything for the glory of God.

1 CORINTHIANS 10:3

How are you currently glorifying God with your body? How could you improve?

One fruit of the Spirit listed in Galatians 5:22–23 is self-control. How might self-control play a role in glorifying God with our bodies?

I understand that keeping our bodies healthy takes intentionality. It takes effort. It takes work. But Galatians 5:16 encourages us in how to succeed: "I say, then, walk by the Spirit and you will certainly not carry out the desire of the flesh." Our flesh will never want what God wants, but He graciously gave us the power of choice. Let's decide together to do all we can to keep our bodies in optimum health so that we can flourish and do all that God has placed us here to do.

PRAY

Leader (or volunteer) read the prayer aloud, or pray independently over your group before closing your time together.

Paul wrote to the Philippians saying much of what he said in his other letters, "My eager expectation and hope is that I will not be ashamed about anything, but that now as always, with all courage, Christ will be highly honored in my body, whether by life or by death" (Philippians 1:20). Like Paul, I feel sure we all want to honor God in our bodies. As we close out our week, let's pray based on this understanding.

Heavenly Father, please help us increase our overall health by taking better care of our temples so we can honor You and glorify You more with them. Help us increase in knowledge of how best to care for our bodies. Please show us strategies for increasing our physical fitness and vitality, and ways to prioritize it in our lives. In Jesus' name, amen.

DAY 5 Guided Prayer and Journaling

But I am like a flourishing olive tree in the house of God;
I trust in God's faithful love forever and ever.
PSALM 52:8

After I had my second baby girl, Sophia, at thirty-nine, I knew I had to get in to shape sooner, rather than later, because I wasn't getting any younger. And I wanted to still be active for when I would be a grandmother . . . especially taking into consideration that most women my age would be great-grandmothers by the time my babies were ready to have babies. I know that sounds like a lot, but that's where my mind went.

When she was about six weeks old, I felt it was time to start, so I mapped out my entire recovery plan. Because I had an unscheduled C-section, I decided that the first week I would crawl around the block, because I was still unsure of standing up straight. No one wants to come apart at the seams—literally. The second week, I would limp around the block. Week three would be a slow walk. Week four a slow jog. And week five, I would finally be running again.

If you're laughing now, you should be. And if you had a C-section, you're even more entitled because you know exactly how unrealistic my plan was.

What I had no clue about was what had actually been done to my abdomen. I'll spare you the details, but the trunk of our bodies is where our core muscles are, the ones that move and stabilize the spine and pelvis. These muscles include the external and deep abdominal muscles, obliques, back muscles, glutes and hip flexors. The pelvic floor and diaphragm can also be considered part of the core, as they play a key role in providing support in the abdomen.[1] Our core muscles literally hold our entire skeletal system in place and affect our ability to stand, lift, twist, turn, move, run, jump, virtually every movement—and they are the muscles that had been cut. Not all of them, of course, but enough that it mattered.

The benefits of a strong core include preventing injuries, reducing back pain, improving posture, lifting efficiency, and athletic performance. A strong core stabilizes the body, allowing us to move in any direction, even on the most uneven terrain (like on a hiking trail), or stand in one spot without losing our balance. Having a strong core lessens our risk of falling.[2] We use our core in the midst of everyday activities all the time—mowing the lawn, taking out the trash, picking up a toddler, unloading the groceries, getting up and down out of an office chair, playing pickleball, or gardening.

I came to understand that if I had a disparity between my inner core and the pressure and weight that I will bear in the future, I could collapse internally in the years to come. I needed to take the time to let my body heal from having Sophia, before strengthening my core. Then I could start all the running I wanted to do.

Learning all this was a lot to take in, but the more I thought about it, the more I began to realize: *Just like we have a physical core, so we have a spiritual core, too—and if there is a disparity between our inner world—our spiritual core—and the pressure we endure externally, then we will collapse.*

God wants us to strengthen our core. If we don't work our spiritual muscles, we will collapse when the stresses of life bear down on us, whether mentally, emotionally, even physically. God wants us to be healthy—spiritually, mentally, emotionally, in our hearts, in our minds, and in our bodies. He wants us to have a strong and healthy core.

So, what exactly is our spiritual core? In Deuteronomy 6:5, Moses wrote: "Love the Lord your God with all your heart, with all your soul, and with all your strength."

In Matthew 22:37, Jesus quoted this verse: "Love the Lord your God with all your heart, with all your soul, and with all your mind."

As you've walked through this week of study, in what part of your core do you need strengthening?

Is it in your heart? Is this where you need healing, wholeness, and freedom from pain?

Is it in your mind? Is this where you need to renew your mind and replace toxic thoughts with God's thoughts?

Is it in your body? Is this where you need to honor God more by treating your body better? By feeding it proper nutrition and exercising it more?

As we close out our week with prayer and journaling, I want you to look back over our week and note what stands out to you in regard to today's questions. If there's a verse you want to memorize, then write it here.

I want you to be still and sit with God. As you do, I believe you'll experience His presence, His guidance, His healing, and His love. By the way, I'm so proud of you. You've worked hard throughout every week of this study. You are becoming like a flourishing olive tree in the house of God!

NOTES

WEEK 6

Fruitfulness in Abiding

GROUP STUDY

Watch

Watch the video for Week 6: Fruitfulness in Abiding, recording your thoughts as you listen.

The entire journey of being rooted, grafted in, and finding peace has been leading to this ultimate purpose: fruitfulness.

What does it truly mean to bear fruit, and what is required of us to produce a harvest that glorifies God?

To produce more and better fruit, every healthy olive tree—and every growing believer—must be pruned.

> *"I am the true vine, and my Father is the [gardener]. Every branch in me that does not bear fruit he takes away, and every branch that does bear fruit he prunes, that it may bear more fruit."*
> **JOHN 15:1–2 ESV**

Pruning is not punitive; it is restorative.

Spiritual fruit is not about busy activity; it is the tangible evidence of Christ's character being formed in us and flowing through us.

Two Types of Fruitfulness:
1. The Fruit of Character (Internal):
Galatians 5:22–23: love, joy, peace, patience, kindness, goodness, faithfulness, gentleness, and self-control. This is about who we are becoming. It is the evidence of our connection to the vine (Christ).

2. The Fruit of Mission (External):
This involves reaching others with the gospel and demonstrating the love of Jesus. It is the natural overflow of our transformed character. We share the light and life of Christ with others.

> *"By their fruit you will recognize them."*
> **MATTHEW 7:16 NIV**

Our fruitfulness is not meant to end with us; it is designed to have a lasting, generational impact.

Discuss

Leader (or volunteer), read the following aloud to the group and follow with the prompts for discussion.

This session concludes our study by focusing on its ultimate purpose: fruitfulness. God identifies His people in Jeremiah 11:16 as "a **flourishing** olive tree, beautiful with well-formed fruit" (emphasis added). And David declares his fruitfulness in Psalm 52:8.

Reflecting on this entire study, how has your understanding of what it means to "flourish" evolved?

What does the idea of being "beautiful with well-formed fruit" mean to you in a practical sense?

A significant portion of our teaching this week centers on John 15, where Jesus explains that the Father prunes every branch that bears fruit so it will become even more fruitful. Pruning is restorative, not punitive.

Describe a time when God pruned something from your life. At the moment, did it feel like a punishment or a loss?

Looking back, how can you now see that His pruning was an act of love intended to produce more fruit in you?

Fruitfulness is not necessarily about achievements or accolades in this life but about becoming more like Jesus. We are called to produce the fruit of Christlike character and Christlike actions.

The session identifies two primary kinds of spiritual fruit: the fruit of character (Galatians 5:22–23) and the fruit of mission (sharing Christ with others).

Which of the fruits of the Spirit—love, joy, peace, patience, kindness, goodness, faithfulness, gentleness, or self-control—is God most actively cultivating in you during this season?

How does developing this internal character give you the confidence and capacity to produce external fruit by reaching others?

Fruitfulness has a generational impact. Our faithfulness today becomes the seed for a spiritual harvest in the lives of our children, families, and communities for years to come.

Who in your life has been a "fruitful branch" whose legacy of faith has directly impacted you?

What is one intentional action you can take this week to invest in the spiritual legacy you will leave for the next generation?

Our final challenge asks us to identify an area where God might be pruning us and to name one person we can share His love with. As we conclude this study together:

In what area are you asking for God's grace to yield to His pruning process?

How can this group pray for you to be a fruitful branch that brings glory to God and blesses others this week?

GROW

Consider these responses to what you've seen and heard today.

- Think of one person you can share the light and life of Christ with this week. This doesn't necessarily mean praying a prayer with them to give their lives to Christ, but befriending them, and demonstrating the love of Jesus in a tangible way.

- Next, pray for them each time they come to mind, and ask God to show you more ways you can continue to consistently encourage them, make their life a little easier, and keep showing them the love of Christ.

PRAY

Leader (or volunteer) read the prayer aloud, or pray independently over your group before closing your time together.

My prayer for you is based on Matthew 7:20, where Jesus said a second time, "So you'll recognize them by their fruit."

Heavenly Father, please help me bear good fruit in my life. Help me walk in the fruit of the Spirit so when people see me and recognize me by my fruit, they'll see and experience You. In Jesus' name I pray, amen.

Next week, we'll conclude our study of the olive tree with a special experience. After six weeks of looking at all things olive, it's time to eat! We'll enjoy a potluck-style "feast" along with a time of reflection and prayer. Use page 221 to plan for this experience.

NOTES

WEEK 6 | Fruitfulness in Abiding

PERSONAL STUDY

The steady rhythm of daily devotion is a vital part of flourishing in your life with Jesus. Set aside time this week to really dig into God's Word. Each day, open yourself up to the Spirit's work in your heart and mind. Then, prayerfully reflect on the beautiful truth He is revealing during this season of new growth.

DAY 1
Fruitfulness Is Painful

DAY 2
Fruitfulness Is Generational

DAY 3
Fruitfulness Is Generous

DAY 4
Fruitfulness Has an Enemy

DAY 5
Guided Prayer and Journaling

DAY 1 Fruitfulness Is Painful

For an olive tree to be healthy and fruitful, it must be pruned. A farmer who tends to his grove must spend time each spring or summer trimming away branches so the canopy opens up to let in airflow—which prevents disease—and so the sunshine can stretch through the limbs of the tree. This increases the fruitfulness of the olive harvest. If the farmer allows the canopy to grow thick and dense, the light can't get through, and the number of olives harvested will be less than it could have been. It's also important that he cuts away any damaged, dead, or diseased branches, or branches that simply are no longer producing fruit. And it's imperative that he disinfects his tools before moving on to prune the next tree, so he doesn't pass along disease.[1]

However, he can't start this annual process until the tree is at least four years old. Before then, it's best the tree be allowed to grow as much as possible. Because the leaves produce the food for the tree, its essential it have plenty for good energy and growth.[2]

What's interesting about olive trees is that because they are resilient. They can handle being cut back hard. "Hard pruning may seem harsh but it is sometimes necessary to rejuvenate an old, neglected or damaged tree."[3] Let that sink in. Even though pruning feels harsh, if the tree isn't pruned, it won't keep producing fruit. Pruning stimulates fruit-bearing.

When I think about all this, and as I've toured olive farms and spoken with a number of farmers who tenderly care for their groves, I can't help but think of how I've been through seasons spiritually when it felt like God was pruning me. And He was doing it with the same goals in mind—so I could bear more fruit in the future. At the time, I didn't care for it. I didn't like it. It was often painful. And I can think of times when people came into my life to learn and grow and then they moved on. Until I understood God's ways more fully, I didn't see this as growth either; I saw it as loss—for them and for me. But now I know, and I welcome such times, as uncomfortable as it is. I have found that just like pruning is a natural cycle for olive trees to keep producing olives for years and years, so is pruning a natural part of our lives as Christ followers . . . so we can keep being spiritually fruitful in every season of our lives.

We're in Week 6 and we're still learning from the olive tree! I told you from the beginning there was so much we would discover.

In the Old Testament, Isaiah spoke of the pruning God does. Read Isaiah 18:5 and fill in the blanks.

For before the harvest, when the blossoming is over and the blossom becomes a ripening grape, he will ____________ ____________ *the shoots with a* ______________________ *knife, and* ____________ ______________ *and* ____________________ *the branches.*

ISAIAH 18:5

Jesus spoke to us about this pruning as well. He called Himself the vine, and us the branches. Read John 15:1–2 and fill in the blanks.

"I am the true __________________, *and my Father is the* __________________. *Every* ______________ ______ *in me that does not produce* __________________ *he* __________________, *and he* __________________ *every branch that produces* __________________ *so that it will produce* __________________ ______________________*."*

JOHN 15:1–2

We listed the fruit of the Spirit from Galatians 5:22–23 in Week 1, but in light of Jesus wanting us to bear more fruit, let's review this passage.

But the fruit of the Spirit is love, joy, peace, patience, kindness, goodness, faithfulness, gentleness, and self-control. The law is not against such things.

GALATIANS 5:22–23

In John 15, Jesus goes on to tell us more about producing fruit. Read the following verse and underline what He tells us to do about fruit and why.

"My Father is glorified by this: that you produce much fruit and prove to be my disciples."
JOHN 15:8

We are called to lead spiritually-fruitful lives. But, according to what Jesus said, we can't produce fruit unless we are pruned.

Prune

The word *prune* as used in John 15 is *kathairō*. It means "to cleanse, i.e. to prune; to expiate:—purge."[4]

Another biblical usage defines it as "to reduce," "shorten," or "thin out."[5]

The dictionary says it literally means "to cut off", or to "eliminat[e] superfluous matter."[6]

We know what it means to purge our closet. Has God ever moved on your heart to purge certain areas of your life? Explain your answer.

When you purged your life of that thing, what was the result or fruit of the purging?

Think of a time when God did the pruning. Write about that time—how it made you feel and what fruit came out of it.

> *"You did not choose me, but I chose you. I appointed you to go and produce fruit and that your fruit should remain, so that whatever you ask the Father in my name, he will give you."*
> **JOHN 15:16**

Based on this verse, who chose and appointed you, and for what reason?

If we combine the understanding of John 15:1–2 with John 15:16, then what has to happen for us to produce fruit that remains?

> *The* Lord *named you a flourishing olive tree, beautiful with well-formed fruit. He has set fire to it, and its branches are consumed with the sound of a mighty tumult.*
> JEREMIAH 11:16

I read this verse and think of all the plans or projects I've worked on that seemed to go up in smoke. Even when, from my perspective, they did bear fruit. And yet, once God was through setting whatever it was on fire, and the smoke cleared, and new growth came, the fruit was much, much better. And it lasted far longer. Even when I didn't see it immediately.

Can you relate? Maybe you gave your life to a job, a ministry, a church, but there came a day when God wanted you to do something new. He wanted you to bear even more fruit, but in a different way. If something comes to mind, describe it here.

Looking back, can you identify that it was God pruning your life? If He were to do that again (and He will) how will you walk through it differently?

God loves us so much and so desires our flourishing in every season, He will never stop pruning us. He wants to see us bear much fruit and fruit that will remain. How important then that we learn the value of being patient in the pruning.

PRAY

Leader (or volunteer) read the prayer aloud, or pray independently over your group before closing your time together.

My prayer for you today is based on John 15:3–4, because the only way we're going to keep being fruitful is to be pruned, and to remain in Jesus: "You are already clean because of the word I have spoken to you. Remain in me, and I in you. Just as a branch is unable to produce fruit by itself unless it remains on the vine, neither can you unless you remain in me."

Heavenly Father, as hard as it feels sometimes, thank You for loving me enough to prune me. Please help me recognize when You are pruning me, and to remember that You are helping me be even more fruitful and flourishing. In Jesus' name, amen.

DAY 2 Fruitfulness Is Generational

Once, when I was speaking at a conference in England, I took some time to walk around the town where I was staying. The sign on one building indicated that it housed the Family History Society for the area. Knowing Nick's mother came to Australia from England, I was naturally curious. Nick is number twelve of thirteen children, and I just knew this little shop would hold all kinds of exciting information about his heritage. And with my interest as an Australian for all things royal, I was sure I'd find some amazing ancestral connection.

Surprisingly enough, I found the name "Caine" quite easily. As much as I'd like to say that titles like Lord, Baron, Knight, or Prince were scattered throughout the family's history, the truth is they did not appear anywhere—but there were plenty of convicted criminals.

It made perfect sense, of course, since convicts were sent to Australia ages ago and all the family history Nick knew about was in Australia, but all my hopes of being connected to royalty were dashed right then and there. Considering my own family's background was full of adultery, abandonment, addiction, and abuse, I couldn't help but think how Nick and I were quite the pair when we married—however, I daresay, when we married in 1996, we changed the course of history.

Nick and I decided that with us, abuse, abandonment, addiction, hopelessness, and defeat would end. We decided that with God's help, we'd start a new bloodline in Jesus that would impact the generations to come with a future full of life and hope and goodness.

Because we'd both fully given our lives to Christ years before we met, we understood the importance of generational thinking. We knew the importance of fruitfulness, of passing on our faith to our children, our extended family, to friends we would make, and to everyone else we would encounter throughout our lives.

We see generational thinking and its fruitfulness throughout Scripture. Psalm 128:1–6 tells us, "How happy is everyone who fears the Lord, who walks in his ways! You will surely eat what your hands have worked for. You will be happy, and it will go well for you. Your wife will be like a fruitful vine within your house, your children, like young olive trees around your table. In this very way the man who fears the Lord will be blessed. May the Lord bless you from Zion, so that you will see the prosperity of Jerusalem all the days of your life and will see your children's children! Peace be with Israel."

As we've seen, the oldest olive trees on the planet have been fruitful for generations. A generation is an average of twenty-five years, so forty generations can occur in a one-thousand-year span.[1] These ancient olive trees have been fruitful for as many as one hundred generations!

I realize none of us will live to be thousands of years old, but we have the potential to be fruitful for at least a few generations.

Have you considered the influence God has given you to be like an olive tree whose fruitfulness reaches both the present generation and the generations to come? How might that impact the way you pray, live, and make decisions?

God is a generational God. Notice how He introduced Himself to Moses in Exodus 3:6: "I am the God of your father, the God of Abraham, the God of Isaac, and the God of Jacob."

When Paul wrote to his young protégé Timothy, he said, "I recall your sincere faith that first lived in your grandmother Lois and in your mother Eunice and now, I am convinced, is in you also" (2 Timothy 1:5).

Look up the following verses and make notes regarding what you discover about generations and generational thinking, particularly when it comes to passing on our faith. (You can also *dig deeper* by looking up Psalm 145:3–5 and Proverbs 4:1–4, 10–15, 20–22.)

PSALM 78:1–8

PSALM 100:5

One more verse will give us insight into what we can pass on down through the generations. Look up Exodus 34:6–7 and summarize what you learn here.

Did you notice that good as well as bad can be passed down through the generations? Nick and I agreed to start a new bloodline, to pass good instead of bad on to our girls and others. For example, I came from a family where everyone yelled—parents, aunts, uncles, cousins, my brothers, and me . . . literally everyone. Granted, Greeks are loud, but I realized a better way as I connected with older, godly women in the church. I contrasted the peace in their homes with the chaos in my own. Now, sometimes the chaos was fun and joyful at a family get-together, but often it was something else. I found that I liked both. I liked the softer touch for every day and the loud raucousness of fun.

What qualities in your family were passed from one generation to the next? What qualities have you instituted that perhaps were new and different? List both below.

THINGS I SEE THAT WERE PASSED DOWN IN MY FAMILY BLOODLINE	THINGS I'VE INSTITUTED IN MY SPIRITUAL BLOODLINE THAT I PASS ON TO OTHERS

God is interested in our fruitfulness and in us passing that fruitfulness on to the generations that come after us. Let us never find ourselves guilty of what Israel experienced serving the Lord throughout the lifetime of Joshua (Judges 2:7–8): "That whole generation was also gathered to their ancestors. After them another generation rose up who did not know the Lord or the works he had done for Israel" (Judges 2:10).

Their lack of legacy wasn't because they didn't know God, but because they weren't intentional about the fruitfulness of their lives being multiplied in others.

If you want to *dig deeper,* look at the following verses and examine the practical ways we can invest in others: 1 Chronicles 22:6–16; Romans 12:13; Ephesians 4:29; Philippians 2:4; 4:9; 2 Corinthians 1:3–4; 1 Thessalonians 2:8; 2 Timothy 1:3; 2:2; and James 1:19.

Take some time to prayerfully reflect on the way you are investing in others for generational fruitfulness:

- Identify three people you believe God has called you to invest in for His purposes.
- List the ways you are already investing in him/her.
- As you review the verses on the previous page, ask God, "What is an additional way that you are calling me to invest in him/her?" Record your answer in the third column.
- Now identify a step you need to take to make that investment. (Example: "Set up a time to meet for coffee to listen. . . .")

NAME	WAYS I AM ALREADY INVESTING	A WAY TO FURTHER INVEST	A STEP TO MAKE THAT INVESTMENT

PRAY

Leader (or volunteer) read the prayer aloud, or pray independently over your group before closing your time together.

Let's be faithful to pass on our faith to the generations coming after us . . . at home, at work, at church, and in our communities. Even when we're old, let's keep thinking of the generations to come: "Even while I am old and gray, God, do not abandon me, while I proclaim your power to another generation, your strength to all who are to come" (Psalm 71:18).

Let's pray today based on this understanding.

Heavenly Father, thank You for transforming my thinking to think generationally. Help me to be spiritually fruitful in my own life and to pass on that fruitfulness to others. Help me to see the next generation around me everywhere I go and give me words of life to share. In Jesus' name, amen.

DAY 3 Fruitfulness Is Generous

For more than a decade, A21 had an office in Kyiv, Ukraine. When the war in Ukraine began in February 2022, we moved our Kyiv team west, all the way to Poland—though as you might recall, the men had to remain behind to help defend Ukraine. In Warsaw, our Zoe Church pastors, Szymon and Kinga, and their church members cared for the women and children of our A21 Ukraine team. They found housing for them, helped enroll the children in school, and assisted them in acclimating to a new culture at a time when they had left everything and everyone they loved behind.

The people of Zoe Church went above and beyond for our A21 team and their families, but the church members didn't stop there. Over the days, weeks, and months that followed, as millions more crossed the border from Ukraine into Poland, like so many Poles, they threw open the doors of their hearts and homes to complete strangers. They gave up their personal comfort and privacy by inviting Ukrainian refugees to live with them.

One couple from the church, Kamil and Anya, took in twelve members of Anya's family. Another took in complete strangers, a family of five. Another took in seven, a mix of friends and friends of friends. Every church member offered to share their home with whomever needed a place to stay.

Wanting to do more, with the help of supporters the church rented five apartments. Then, a church member rented more apartments, organizing accommodations for up to one hundred people. More church members stepped up with generous hearts and open hands, collecting or purchasing food, diapers, baby formula, clothing, blankets, anything that could help. A team of volunteers went to work helping the refugees find housing, secure medical services, acquire jobs, and get their children enrolled in school.

You may have heard about other such extraordinary acts of kindness on the news; Nick and I did, and we heard it firsthand from Szymon and Kinga, and their team. I remember asking Kinga why she thought the Polish people were so open and generous, despite the natural concerns. A glance back at history said it all: Occupied Poland was home to six death camps during World War II. Kinga said everyone grew up hearing about them at home and at school.

She said to me, "We know the stories. Everyone hid someone. Everyone helped someone escape. My grandparents had stories. My great aunts and uncles had stories. How could we not glance back at the past and do it again? When the war came, we knew what to do. It was natural for us."

Imagining this happening where I live, I found myself wondering if the people in my city would be just as willing to throw open their doors and share their most sacred spaces. I couldn't help but ask myself if Nick and I would do it as quickly as the people of Zoe Church did. I hope so, but it made me more aware than ever that I want to be a person who is willing to share what I have and be generous all the time, wherever I live and with whomever I encounter. I don't want to wait until there is a crisis to be generous, or until I think I have enough to share, and I imagine neither do you.

Looking at your life and habits, how would you rate yourself as a generous person?

1	2	3	4	5	6	7	8	9	10

I could be more generous. *I am freely and consistently generous.*

How are you most generous? What comes easily to you? Circle those below.

Time	Possessions	Words	Gifts	Energy
Money	Talents	Knowledge	Wisdom	

In what ways do you want to be more generous? Put a box around the ones above.

I can understand, perhaps because of our background, or experiences we've lived through—particularly those involving scarcity—we feel a need to hold tightly to whatever resources God has given to us. But the Word shows us over and over again to hold what we have loosely, to freely give, and to have a generous attitude.

Look up Proverbs 11:24–25 in the NIV and write it here.

In the New Testament church, the people pooled their resources to ensure everyone had enough: "They sold their possessions and property and distributed the proceeds to all, as any had need" (Acts 2:45). I'm not sure how doable that is in our day and age, but it is possible to give each time we have an opportunity to be generous, whether that be sharing a meal, practicing hospitality, or throwing open wide the doors of our hearts and homes.

Generosity

Generosity is "the free and liberal bestowal of wealth, possessions or food upon others. The generosity of God is shown in his free bestowal of grace upon undeserving sinners."[1]

The man with a "generous heart" (*nadiyb libbo*) in Ex. 35:5 is one who gives willingly, and Heb. hānan means especially to deal graciously with the needy but undeserving.[2]

The Greek term "*agathós* can be used for any good characteristic, *koinōnikós* specifically denotes giving what is one's own, and *aphelótēs, haplōs*, and *haplótēs* emphasize sincerity in giving."[3]

Did you have the opportunity to be generous in the last week? Describe your experience here.

Not only does God want us to be generous, our attitude matters to Him. Read 2 Corinthians 9:6–7 and underline the attitude that God wants us to give to others.

The person who sows sparingly will also reap sparingly, and the person who sows generously will also reap generously. Each person should do as he has decided in his heart—not reluctantly or out of compulsion, since God loves a cheerful giver.
2 CORINTHIANS 9:6–7

Read what God tells us in the verse that follows. Underline each time the word *every/everything* is used.

And God is able to make every grace overflow to you, so that in every way, always having everything you need, you may excel in every good work.
2 CORINTHIANS 9:8

In the ESV, the phrase "so that in every way" reads "so that having all sufficiency." The Greek word translated as "sufficiency" is *autarkeia*. Its meaning encompasses the idea of "a perfect condition of life in which no aid or support is needed."[4] In light of this, look back at verse 6, "The person who sows sparingly will also reap sparingly, and the person who sows generously will also reap generously." God supplies everything we need when we're generous—and when we're generous, God gives us more so we can continue to give.[5]

God makes us fruitful so we can be generous. Why then is it that we often wait until we have what we think is enough to give, to serve, to invest our time, talent, and treasure?

If you want to *go deeper*, look up the following verses to discover more about how God is generous with us. Then, match up the verse references with what you discover by drawing lines from one to the other.

PROVERBS 20:24	He gives us rest.
MATTHEW 11:29–30	He gives us an escape from temptation.
EPHESIANS 2:10	He gives us provision.
PHILIPPIANS 4:19	He gives us direction.
1 CORINTHIANS 10:13	He gives us purpose and works to do.
1 TIMOTHY 6:17	He gives us peace.
PHILIPPIANS 4:7	He provides us with good things to enjoy.

Ephesians 3:20–21 give us yet one more powerful glimpse into God's generous ways.

> *Now to Him who is able to do exceedingly abundantly above all that we ask or think, according to the power that works in us, to Him be glory in the church by Christ Jesus to all generations, forever and ever. Amen.*
> **EPHESIANS 3:20–21 NKJV**

Exceedingly.

Abundantly.

Above all we could ask or think.

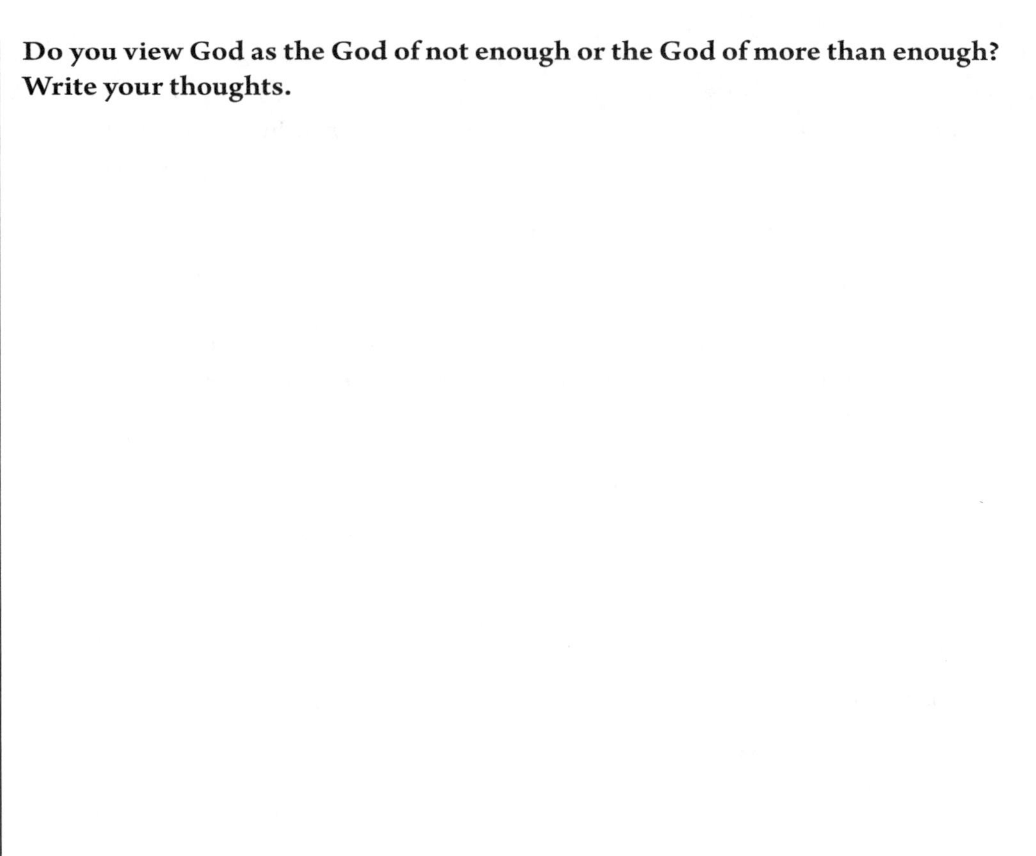

Do you view God as the God of not enough or the God of more than enough? Write your thoughts.

The earth is the Lord's and all that is in it (Psalm 24:1–2; 50:10–12), so how could He not have enough to give us? "What no eye has seen, no ear has heard, and no human heart has conceived—God has prepared these things for those who love him" (1 Corinthians 2:9).

Read Luke 6:38 here and answer the questions that follow.

> *"Give, and it will be given to you; a good measure—pressed down, shaken together, and running over—will be poured into your lap. For with the measure you use, it will be measured back to you."*
>
> LUKE 6:38

What does God say for us to do?

What will happen if we do give?

How will it be given to us?

What does "with the measure you use, it will be measured back to you" mean?

Olive trees keep on producing year after year, no matter how many years they live. We are like olive trees in the house of God! And fruitful people are generous people!

Each day, we want to look for ways to be generous with what God has entrusted to us. Proverbs 3:27 is one more verse we can keep in mind as we do: "Do not withhold good from those to whom it is due, When it is in the power of your hand to do so" (NKJV).

PRAY

Leader (or volunteer) read the prayer aloud, or pray independently over your group before closing your time together.

As we close our day in prayer, let's remember the words of Paul in Acts 20:35, "In every way I've shown you that it is necessary to help the weak by laboring like this and to remember the words of the Lord Jesus, because he said, 'It is more blessed to give than to receive.'"

And let's not forget how important it is for us to be as willing to receive as we are to give. Ouch. I know. I imagine we all feel more comfortable giving than receiving but receiving is how we started our Christian walk, and it's one more component of how we're to walk like Christ.

Heavenly Father, please help us to be mindful of others, always. To be generous and give of our time, energy, talents, treasure, resources, knowledge, and wisdom. Help us to recognize all that You give us, and to freely share it with others. In Jesus' name, amen.

DAY 4 Fruitfulness Has an Enemy

On the rare occasions when normally resilient olive trees begin to show symptoms of sickness or infestation, there is one culprit in particular that a farmer will always be on the lookout for because it is an especially difficult enemy to fight—the olive fruit fly.

No bigger than about three-sixteenths of an inch, the olive fruit fly, if not controlled, is capable of destroying one hundred percent of a grove's crop.

No wonder farmers are on the alert year-round. Not to give you an entomology lesson, but to help increase our understanding of this pest: Typically, in the Spring, an adult olive fruit fly lays its eggs in unharvested fruit from the previous year's crop. When the larvae hatch, they feed exclusively on the fruit. Then, as they grow, they become a threat to the new crop of olives appearing on the trees.

If a farmer spots any of these pests, then he or she knows to take action quickly. To control potential infestations, there are a number of methods farmers can use, including preventative ones.

I won't get into the pros or cons of all these methods as I'm not an expert on such matters, but I fully understand that for anyone managing a grove anywhere in the world, the fight against the olive fruit fly has to be ongoing and intentional. A farmer can't fight this enemy of the olive tree once and then forget about it; its threat is all too real throughout the life of the tree.[1]

Understanding this, I can't help but think of how we're called to be flourishing olive trees, and we, too, have an enemy. His name is Satan (1 Chronicles 21:1), and he is a very real adversary. Like the olive fruit fly, he's ever ready to interfere in the fruitfulness of our lives.

You and I are here to fight the good fight of faith, to go and make disciples, to be salt and light in a dark world—and the enemy will always do whatever he can to get us sidetracked.

Maybe you've felt him needling around in your life lately. He's a master at using distractions, pointless arguments, and negative thoughts to tempt us away from fulfilling our purpose and walking in all the fruitfulness God has for us.

Thankfully, he is also a defeated foe. Jesus defeated him personally by overcoming his trickery, treachery, and temptations (Luke 4); casting out demons (Matthew 12:28); healing a woman bound by him (Luke 13:16), and more. Ultimately, Jesus was crucified, buried, raised, and seated at the right hand of the Father, defeating the enemy, making a way for us to be forgiven of our sin, brought into relationship with God, and filled with the Holy Spirit.

Read the following verses to discover how Jesus defeated the enemy and why the enemy has no power over us.

"Look, I have given you the authority to trample on snakes and scorpions and over all the power of the enemy; nothing at all will harm you."
LUKE 10:19

He has rescued us from the domain of darkness and transferred us into the kingdom of the Son he loves.
COLOSSIANS 1:13

He disarmed the rulers and authorities and disgraced them publicly; he triumphed over them in him.
COLOSSIANS 2:15

You are from God, little children, and you have conquered them, because the one who is in you is greater than the one who is in the world.
1 JOHN 4:4

Because we live in the *already-and-not-yet* when God's kingdom has already broken in but is not yet here in its fullness, the prince of the power of the air is still at work (Ephesians 2:2). We fight against him in the good fight of faith (2 Timothy 4:7). While we are saved and filled with God's Spirit, we still have to contend with our enemy and his mission to thwart our fruitfulness.

There are a number of verses that describe our enemy and expose his behavior and strategies. Look up the following verses and fill in the blanks.

"When he tells a lie, he speaks from his own nature, because he is a ________________ and the ________________ of ________________."
JOHN 8:44

And you were dead in your trespasses and sins in which you previously walked according to the ways of this world, according to the ________________ of the ________________ of the ________________, the ________________ now working in the disobedient.
EPHESIANS 2:1–2

> *Be sober-minded, be alert. Your ____________________ the ____________________ is prowling around ____________________ a roaring lion, looking for ____________________ he can devour.*
>
> 1 PETER 5:8

Our enemy was originally known as Lucifer (Ezekiel 28; Isaiah 14:12), an angel created by God, who rebelled and was cast down to the earth (Luke 10:18). We know him by many names.

Looking back at the verses you read, make a list of the words and phrases used to describe our enemy.

No matter what we call our enemy, he has one overarching mission. Read John 10:10 and list three ways he attempts to carry out his mission.

1.
2.
3.

The enemy does not want us to thrive or flourish. Thankfully, we have authority in Jesus to remind him that he is defeated, to come against him, and to overcome his work in our lives.

God has equipped us to do this in several ways. According to James 4:7, we're to submit to God, resist the devil, and he will flee from us.

God has also given us spiritual armor to wear in our fight (Ephesians 6:11–17).

Let's walk through each of these pieces:

1. ***The Belt of Truth:*** The enemy is the father of lies, so we must understand, speak, and walk in the truth (3 John 4) to overcome his lies.

2. ***The Breastplate of Righteousness:*** We have been made the righteousness of God in Christ Jesus (2 Corinthians 5:21). We are in right standing with Him, so the enemy's condemnation that we are orphans, not accepted, unloved, etc. are overcome.

3. ***Our Feet Sandaled with the Gospel of Peace:*** Through Jesus Christ, we have peace with God (Romans 5:1). As we carry the gospel into enemy territory, and people respond by accepting Jesus as their Lord and Savior, those who are enemies of God become children of God and the enemy is overcome.

4. ***The Shield of Faith:*** "Faith comes by hearing, and hearing by the word of God" (Romans 10:17 NKJV). By confident assurance of God's faithfulness and Word, we overcome the enemy's attempts to get us to walk by sight.

5. ***The Helmet of Salvation:*** The enemy accuses us, pointing out how we fall short, even calling our salvation into question. Being anchored in the truth of who our Savior is and what He has done renders the enemy ineffective.

6. ***The Sword of the Spirit:*** Reading, memorizing, praying, declaring, and obeying God's Word, we wield it as a sword against the enemy, overcoming his temptations and lies.

One more thing: Did you notice that our struggle is not against flesh and blood, which is other people, but against the spiritual forces of our enemy? When challenges come our way, this is what we sometimes forget; and instead of fighting our enemy, we fight one another.

How many times have we seen people slug it out on social media? How many times have we seen people post their opinions, the kind that tear down instead of build up? If we jump in that kind of fray, we'll take ourselves out of the right fight and engage ourselves in the wrong one. Regardless of what people might do to us, they are not our enemy. The evil one is.

In Ephesians 6:18–20, Paul continues with a very important point. Read the following verses and circle the word *pray* or *prayer* every time you see it.

> *Pray at all times in the Spirit with every prayer and request, and stay alert with all perseverance and intercession for all the saints. Pray also for me, that the message may be given to me when I open my mouth to make known with boldness the mystery of the gospel. For this I am an ambassador in chains. Pray that I might be bold enough to speak about it as I should.*
>
> EPHESIANS 6:18–20

Prayer is the weapon of our warfare, availing us to God's power, strengthening us to endure in the face of struggle. James wrote that the prayers of the righteous have great power (James 5:16).

Understanding all that you do now about how the enemy can come against us, can you identify ways the enemy has been coming against you lately?

List some ways we can overcome the enemy in our lives. Think back to Week 5 Day 3, where we studied renewing our minds with the truth. When we renew our minds, we defeat him and his influence in our lives.

Remember how I said I used to skip ballet class to play soccer across the street with the boys? Well, my antics worked until Mum caught on, and then she told all my aunts because nothing in our family was ever private. In our family, if one person knew, then fifty knew—and everyone felt the freedom to speak to you about anything, including skipping ballet.

I remember when one of my aunts spoke her mind. I feel sure she meant well, but what she said affected me deeply. "Christine," she said, "you should prefer ballet to soccer. You're not feminine enough."

Though it was years before I was mature enough to process what she actually said, the message was clear because it included that all too familiar word "enough." I had heard it for years. Not good enough. Not smart enough. And now, not feminine enough. Her words became one more lie of the enemy that I believed about myself because, until I turned my life over to God, I didn't know how to defeat such lies. I remember how I even took up repeating the lies to myself and to others. Isn't that what we do when we don't realize the enemy's work? I can remember saying things like, "No one will ever love me," or, "I'm a failure," or "I'm damaged goods."

Have you ever said such negative things? I imagine that if we heard one of our daughters or friends saying such things, we'd be so quick to interrupt with affirming words of love and life, wouldn't we? And yet, until we know better, it's so easy to mistakenly join in the enemy's chorus. Remember, Jesus said that Satan is the father of lies and accuser of us all. When he lies, he speaks his native tongue, and when we join in with those lies, it seems all our emotions and feelings follow along. It seems to only reinforce what's not true.

When I began to learn what God said and thought about me, and when I began to believe it and then say it, my life changed. To realize that I shouldn't believe all my feelings and thoughts, especially when they contradicted the Word of God, was a game changer.

I don't know what lies are tormenting you today, but to keep being a flourishing, fruitful olive tree, you will need to put a stop to them by replacing them with the absolute truth of God's Word. Sure, you'll still hear the enemy speaking his lies, but you won't ever have to believe them or repeat them again.

As we end our day, I want to remind you of the encouraging words of Romans 8:31, 37–39. Because of Jesus, no matter what comes against us, we are more than conquerors in him.

What, then, are we to say about these things? If God is for us, who is against us? . . . No, in all these things we are more than conquerors through him who loved us. For I am persuaded that neither death nor life, nor angels nor rulers, nor things present nor things to come, nor powers, nor height nor depth, nor any other created thing will be able to separate us from the love of God that is in Christ Jesus our Lord.

ROMANS 8:31, 37–39

PRAY

Leader (or volunteer) read the prayer aloud, or pray independently over your group before closing your time together.

Congratulations! You did it! I'm so proud of you. You have been faithful and diligent through every week of our study, and I'm confident that you'll never forget the meaningfulness of the olive tree in Scripture—or the fact that you are like a flourishing olive tree in the house of God who trusts in His faithful love forever and ever (Psalm 52:8)!

Let's close in prayer, thanking God for all He's done in us and through us in our time together.

Heavenly Father, thank You for all we have learned, and for all You've done in us and through us during this study. Please help us to keep flourishing in fulfilling all the plans and purpose You have for us, and with reaching others with the good news of Your saving grace. Help us to remember who we are—olive trees—and what we're called to do—be fruitful. In Jesus' name, amen.

DAY 5 Guided Prayer and Journaling

But I am like a flourishing olive tree in the house of God;
I trust in God's faithful love forever and ever.
PSALM 52:8

Jesus said in John 15:5, "The one who remains in me and I in him produces much fruit."

In John 15:8, He said, "My Father is glorified by this: that you produce much fruit and prove to be my disciples."

And in John 15:16, He said, "You did not choose me, but I chose you. I appointed you to go and produce fruit and that your fruit should remain, so that whatever you ask the Father in my name, he will give you."

Clearly, we were created to be fruitful. When we are born again, we are called to bear much spiritual fruit for the glory of God. But to become fruitful and to remain fruitful, we will have to remain in Christ.

In John 15:4, Jesus said, "Remain in me, and I in you. Just as a branch is unable to produce fruit by itself unless it remains on the vine, neither can you unless you remain in me."

Today is our guided prayer and journaling day. It's our day to sit at His feet. To worship. To contemplate. To record our thoughts. I hope as you've experienced these days, you've enjoyed them. Sometimes, we need to stop doing and just be.

In Galatians 5:22–25, God gave us the nine fruits of the Spirit—a list by which we can keep in touch with nine aspects of our fruitfulness.

But the fruit of the Spirit is love, joy, peace, patience, kindness, goodness, faithfulness, gentleness, and self-control. The law is not against such things. Now those who belong to Christ Jesus have crucified the flesh with its passions and desires. If we live by the Spirit, let us also keep in step with the Spirit.
GALATIANS 5:22–25

In a world full of pain, suffering, chaos, arguing, strife, and division, I imagine we need a little more love, joy, peace, patience, kindness, goodness, faithfulness, gentleness, and self-control, don't we? Somehow, I feel our world would be a very different place if the followers of Jesus released more of this fruit of the Spirit into the world.

I think one of the most effective witnessing tools in our generation could be the people of God reflecting the character of God in a world that lives so antithetically to the ways of God. The fruit of the Spirit is what every Jesus follower should be producing, and it should make a difference in our homes, families, friendships, communities, workplaces, and world. We are supposed to be like green olive trees in our world, producing well-formed fruit that would cause an unbelieving neighbor to ask us, "Why are you so different?"

> **As we sit and think and pray today, let's think on these nine ways we can be fruitful in our inner world, in our relationships, in our influence.**

Imagine if we started right where we are, spreading . . .

Love in the midst of indifference.

Joy in the midst of sorrow.

Peace in the midst of chaos.

Patience in the midst of frenzy.

Kindness in the midst of cruelty.

Goodness in the midst of selfishness.

Faithfulness in the midst of carelessness.

Gentleness in the midst of hardness.

Self-control in the midst of a world spiraling out of control.

Remember to bring a dish to share with your group this week! Preview the questions on pages 210–211 in order to make the most of your experience.

WEEK 7

Feasting Together

GROUP STUDY

Watch

Watch the video for Week 7: Feasting Together, recording your thoughts as you listen.

The "Eat Everything" Philosophy:
Greek cultural emphasizes food and celebration. Physical feasting is connected to a spiritual desire: to leave not just with a full stomach, but with a **full heart**, fired up for God's purposes.

The Core Commission:
"I am like a flourishing olive tree in the house of God." (Psalm 52:8)

Main Goal: To go out and flourish like olive trees in a world that desperately needs rootedness and connection.

Remember: Olive trees do not wilt in adversity. Abounding comes from **abiding**. We flourish not because of easy circumstances, but because of what we are rooted in: **His Presence**.

Contrast:
Pride: Distances us from God, relies on self, and seeks to serve its own interests.

Humility: Draws near to God, relies on prayer, and seeks to serve others.

Key Statement: "There is no greater foe of grace and growth than spiritual pride." Biblical peacemakers are not passive. They seek God's perspective ("What do You see?") and practice removing barriers between "what is" and "what God wants to be."

Reframing Pain:
Many equate pressing with abandonment or defeat. Jesus engaged the pressing with **submission and surrender** (Luke 22:42), anchored in the Father's goodness.

The Pathway:
The entrance to the "highway of happiness" is the **fear of the Lord**. Fearing God leads to obedience; obedience turns us from the anxiety and weight of sin, leading to true flourishing.

The Mandate:
God has purposed us for a life of eternal impact, not little impact. Jesus promised we would bear "**much fruit**" if we remain in Him. Heroes of the faith did not flourish by their own strength; they flourished because they **remained rooted**.

Discuss and Experience

Leader (or volunteer), read the following aloud to the group and follow with the prompts for discussion.

This final week has been set aside for reflection and celebration as a group. A vital part of Christian flourishing is to enjoy God together—praising Him for His abundant goodness. We see this in the description of the earliest church. The first Christians were rooted in Christ, even in challenging circumstances, and they experienced the Holy Spirit moving in and through them. Isn't this the kind of flourishing we crave?

> *They devoted themselves to the apostles' teaching, to the fellowship, to the breaking of bread, and to prayer. . . . They ate their food with joyful and sincere hearts, praising God and enjoying the favor of all the people. Every day the Lord added to their number those who were being saved.*
>
> ACTS 2:42, 46–47

Start by allowing a moment for everyone to tell the group about the olive-related dish they've provided.

What did you bring and why did you bring it? (Is it a personal favorite, a sentimental recipe, something new to try, or maybe even something inspired by this study?)

Next, provide three simple instructions for the meal—whether it's a snack or a feast.

1. *Invite everyone to go get what they'd like to eat and drink.*
2. *Encourage people to taste something they might not usually try. (After all, everyone isn't raised on olives by a Greek mum!)*
3. *Emphasize the importance of savoring the unique qualities of whatever they're sampling.*

Finally, as everyone enjoys this time of food and fellowship among friends, ask the following questions.

What quality stands out most to you in the olive-inspired dishes you've tasted? Is there imagery or a lesson to be gleaned from these flavors or characteristics—either reinforcing or adding to something from the past six weeks?

How has this study of the olive tree encouraged you spiritually? Which week was especially meaningful to you? (Each person should check one box for the closing prayer time.)

- [ ] Week 1: Rooted in God's Presence
- [ ] Week 2: Grafted into the Family
- [ ] Week 3: Branches of Peace
- [ ] Week 4: Oil from Pressing
- [ ] Week 5: Growing in Health
- [ ] Week 6: Fruitfulness in Abiding

GROW

Consider what you've seen and heard today and take action in your daily life applying this truth.

In every season of life, there are certain practices we want to engage in regularly to cultivate healthy spiritual growth. Over time, these ongoing rhythms help us remain rooted in Christ.

- Identify ways to begin developing steady rhythms in your life—no matter what season you're in. What practices might work for you?

PRAY

Leader (or volunteer) read the prayer aloud, or pray independently over your group before closing your time together.

Conclude your study of the olive tree with the following prayer experience.

- *Explain that you will read the prayers mentioned in the video, pausing after each one.*
- *Invite each person who chose that week as especially meaningful to voice a two-sentence prayer, personalizing it and asking God to answer that prayer in their lives. For example: "God you ______. Help me to ______."*
- *End by asking each person to voice the final prayer for Week 7.*

I am praying…

1. You flourish as one who is rooted and resilient in Jesus' name.
2. You flourish in humility.
3. God would use you to powerfully bring His peace everywhere you go.
4. You flourish in the place of pressing.
5. You flourish in God's happiness.
6. You flourish in producing much fruit.
7. You root and remain.

Endnotes

Introduction

1. "Parthenon," History, updated May 2025, https://www.history.com/articles/parthenon #Athena-Parthenos.

2. "The Parthenon: The Creation Of A Masterpiece," Athens Walking Tours Travelogue, September 5, 2013, https://www.athenswalkingtours.gr/blog/2013/09/05/the-creation -of-a-masterpiece/.

3. Sign 8 at the Acropolis.

4. "The Sacred Athena Olive Tree on Top of the Acropolis," Athens Walking Tours Travelogue, October 31, 2012, https://www.athenswalkingtours.gr/blog/2012/10/31/the-sacred-olive -tree/.

5. Regina Gagnon, "The Two Olive Trees," *Great Works of Literature I (Fall 2016)* (blog), September 6, 2016, https://blogs.baruch.cuny.edu/greatworks2016/?p=179.

WEEK 1 Day 1

1. "Olive Tree Roots: Everything You Need to Know," Greg, last modified July 20, 2024, https://greg.app/olive-tree-roots/.

2. "8 Amazing Attributes of Olive Trees That Will Humble and Inspire You," Olive My Pickle, accessed January 28, 2026, https://www.olivemypickle.com/blogs/news/8-amazing -attributes-of-olive-trees-that-will-humble-and-inspire-you.

3. "8 Amazing Attributes of Olive Trees."

4. *Merriam-Webster Dictionary*, "root," last updated January 25, 2026, https://www.merriam -webster.com/dictionary/root.

5. *Dictionary.com*, "rooting," accessed January 28, 2026, https://www.dictionary.com/browse /rooting#:~:text=the%20process%20of%20propagating%20plants,can%20be%20done %20in%20water.

6. *Dictionary.com*, "rooted," accessed January 28, 2026, https://www.dictionary.com/browse /rooted.

WEEK 1 Day 2

1. Ken Goldstein, "The Janka Hardness Test for Hardwoods," The Iaido Journal, April 2009, https://ejmas.com/tin/2009tin/tinart_goldstein_0904.html.

2. "Olive Wood - Characteristics, Uses and Benefits," Wood Assistant, accessed January 28, 2026, http://www.woodassistant.com/wood-database/olive-wood/.

3. *Holman Illustrated Bible Dictionary*, Chad Brand et al., eds., (Holman Bible Publishers, 2003), under "Increase."

4. *Merriam-Webster Dictionary*, "wisdom," last updated January 28, 2026, https://www .merriam-webster.com/dictionary/wisdom.

5. C. Hassell Bullock, "Wisdom," in *Evangelical Dictionary of Biblical Theology*, (Baker Book House, 1996).

6. *Holman Illustrated Bible Dictionary*, Chad Brand et al., eds., (Holman Bible Publishers, 2003), under "Stature."

7. *Evangelical Dictionary of Biblical Theology*, (Holman Bible Publishers, 2003), under "Favor."

WEEK 1 Day 3

1. "Olive grove enviroment & natural biodiversity," Mavroudis, accessed January 28, 2026, https://oliveoilcorfu.gr/olive-grove-enviroment-natural-biodiversity/.
2. David Feela, "Neighbors who visit my backyard in the dead of night," High Country News, April 23, 2014, https://www.hcn.org/wotr/neighbors-who-visit-my-backyard-in-the-dead-of-night/.
3. "Our Coratina and Peranzana olive trees in defense of the environment," Oilalà, June 3, 2021, https://www.oilala.com/en/the-olive-tree-and-its-important-role-in-the-protection-of-the-environment/.
4. *Merriam-Webster Dictionary*, "shade," last updated January 27, 2026, https://www.merriam-webster.com/dictionary/shade.

WEEK 1 Day 4

1. Beth, "Choosing the Best Olive Tree: The Ultimate Guide," Olive Grove Oundle, March 27, 2024 , https://www.olivegroveoundle.co.uk/choosing-best-olive-tree/.
2. Leslie C. Allen, "Glory," in *The Lexham Bible Dictionary*, John D. Barry, et al., eds., (Lexham Press, 2016).
3. *Bible Sense Lexicon*, Logos Bible Software, 2009, under "beauty ⇔ glory."
4. *Holman Illustrated Bible Dictionary*, Chad Brand et al., eds., (Holman Bible Publishers, 2003), under "Glory."
5. John Piper, host, *Ask Pastor John*, podcast, episode 390, "What Is God's Glory?," Desiring God, July 22, 2014, https://www.desiringgod.org/interviews/what-is-gods-glory--2.
6. Matthew Henry, *Matthew Henry's Concise Commentary on the Bible*, on 1 Samuel 16:7 and 1 Peter 3:1–7, Christian Classics Ethereal Library, PDF, accessed January 29, 2026, https://ccel.org/ccel/h/henry/mhcc/cache/mhcc.pdf; Charles Spurgeon, "The Beauty of the Olive Tree", no. 3176, sermon, Metropolitan Tabernacle, London, England, April 17, 1879, published December 16, 1909, Christian Classic Ethereal Library, https://ccel.org/ccel/spurgeon/sermons55/sermons55.lii.html.

WEEK 1 Day 5

1. *Oxford English Dictionary*, "linger," last updated December 2025, https://www.oed.com/dictionary/linger_v?tab=meaning_and_use#39235844.

WEEK 2 Introduction/Video

1. Mark McWhorter, "The Grafted Olive Tree," Wisdom's Corner (blog), The Old Paths Bible School, 2002, http://www.oldpaths.org/Classes/Children/WC/Stories/wc06_15.html.

WEEK 2 Day 1

1. "Social Media and Self Esteem: The Rise of Social Media," D'Amore Mental Health, accessed January 28, 2026, https://damorementalhealth.com/social-media-and-self-esteem#:~:text=One%20study%20found%20that%20adolescents,self%2Dimage%2C%20and%20loneliness.
2. List inspired by: Connie Thompson, "Jesus and the Outcasts: 5 Groups Who Felt God's Love," Jesus Film Project, December 8, 2017, https://www.jesusfilm.org/blog/outcasts-jesus-loved/.

WEEK 2 Day 2

1. Bible Hub, "Grace," accessed January 28, 2026, https://bibleapps.com/g/grace.htm.
2. J. Hampton Keathley III, "Grace and Peace," Bible.org, April 22, 2005, https://bible.org/article/grace-and-peace.
3. *Evangelical Dictionary of Biblical Theology*, (Holman Bible Publishers, 2003), under "Grace."
4. Matthew Henry, *Matthew Henry's Concise Commentary on the Bible*, on Ephesians 2:1–10, Classics Ethereal Library, PDF, accessed January 29, 2026, https://ccel.org/ccel/h/henry/mhcc/cache/mhcc.pdf.
5. See marginal note in the Christian Standard Bible.

WEEK 2 Day 3

1. Gary Hardin, "Humility," in *Holman Illustrated Bible Dictionary*, Chad Brand, et al., eds., (Holman Bible Publishers, 2003).
2. *Oxford English Dictionary*, "entitlement," last updated September 2025, https://www.oed.com/dictionary/entitlement_n?tab=meaning_and_use#31518010.
3. This quotation is often misattributed to C. S. Lewis, who wrote something similar in *Mere Christianity* (chap. 8) but you can find it in Rick Warren's *The Purpose-Driven Life* (day 19).
4. N. J. Opperwall, "Low; Lowly," in *The International Standard Bible Encyclopedia*, rev. ed., Geoffrey W Bromiley, ed., (Eerdmans, 1979–1988).

WEEK 2 Day 4

1. A rendition of this story first appeared in Christine Caine, *Unexpected: Leave Fear Behind, Move Forward in Faith, Embrace the Adventure* (Zondervan, 2018), chap. 4.
2. *Merriam-Webster Dictionary*, "prejudice," last updated January 28, 2026, https://www.merriam-webster.com/dictionary/prejudice.
3. *Merriam-Webster Dictionary*, "prejudice."
4. *Merriam-Webster Dictionary*, "everyone," accessed January 28, 2026, https://www.merriam-webster.com/dictionary/everyone.

WEEK 3 Day 1

1. Joshua M. Greever, "Peace," in *The Lexham Bible Dictionary*, John D. Barry, et al., eds., (Lexham Press, 2016).
2. Stan Norman, "Reconciliation," in *Holman Illustrated Bible Dictionary*, Chad Brand et al., eds., (Holman Bible Publishers, 2003).

WEEK 3 Day 3

1. *Merriam-Webster Dictionary*, "conflict," last updated January 23, 2026, https://www.merriam-webster.com/dictionary/conflict.
2. *Merriam-Webster Dictionary*, "strife," last updated January 23, 2026, https://www.merriam-webster.com/dictionary/strife.
3. *Holman Illustrated Bible Dictionary*, Chad Brand et al., eds., (Holman Bible Publishers, 2003), under "Peacemakers."

WEEK 3 Day 4

1. "Greece plans Turkey border fence to tackle migration," BBC, January 4, 2011, https://www.bbc.com/news/world-europe-12109595.

2. Ronald Lowe, "The accountability and Responsibility of the Church," Sermons by Logos, 2021, https://sermons.logos.com/sermons/745846-the-accountability-and-responsibility-ofthe-church.

WEEK 4 Introduction/Video

1. T. D. Alexander, "Jesus as Messiah," The Gospel Coalition, accessed February 12, 2026, https://www.thegospelcoalition.org/essay/jesus-as-messiah/.

2. See Christine Caine, *How Did I Get Here? Finding Your Way Back to God When Everything Is Pulling You Away* (Thomas Nelson, 2021), chap. 9.

3. "Gethsemane Definition," That the World May Know with Ray Vander Laan, accessed February 12, 2026, https://www.thattheworldmayknow.com/define-gethsemane#:~:text=The%20word%20gethsemane%20is%20derived,crushed%20in%20an%20olive%20crusher.

WEEK 4 Day 1

1. "Buckingham Palace publishes Order of Service for the Coronation of The King and Queen," Westminster Abbey, May 6, 2023, https://www.westminster-abbey.org/abbey-news/buckingham-palace-publishes-order-of-service-for-the-coronation-of-the-king-and-queen.

2. Noah Hurowitz, "Opinion: The hidden meaning in the anointing of King Charles," CNN, May 3, 2023, https://www.cnn.com/2023/05/03/opinions/opinion-the-hidden-meaning-in-the-anointing-of-king-charles-hurowitz.

3. "A guide to coronations," Westminster Abbey, accessed January 28, 2026, https://www.westminster-abbey.org/history/coronations-at-the-abbey/a-guide-to-coronations.

4. Meredith Faubel Nyberg, "Anointing," in *The Lexham Bible Dictionary*, John D. Barry, et al., eds., (Lexham Press, 2016).

5. Nyberg, "Anointing."

6. Mark L. Strauss, "Messiah," in *The Lexham Bible Dictionary*, John D. Barry, et al., eds., (Lexham Press, 2016).

WEEK 4 Day 2

1. "Jesus Teaches about Salt and Light," Mission Bible Class, accessed January 28, 2026, https://missionbibleclass.org/new-testament/part1/parables-teachings-of-jesus/jesus-teaches-about-salt-and-light/.

WEEK 4 Day 3

1. Cris Hazzard, "Mount Baden-Powell Hike," HikingGuy (blog), last updated January 19, 2025, https://hikingguy.com/hiking-trails/los-angeles-hikes/mount-baden-powell-hike/.

2. *Bible Sense Lexicon*, Logos Bible Software, 2009, under "advocate (legal)."

3. *Bible Sense Lexicon*, "advocate (legal)."

4. Rick Brannan, *Lexham Research Lexicon of the Greek New Testament*, (Lexham Press, 2020), under paraklētos.

5. "Zechariah," Christianity.com, accessed January 28, 2026, https://www.christianity.com/bible/niv/zechariah/.

WEEK 4 Day 4

1. "How to Taste Olive Oil Like a Pro," Bona Furtuna, accessed January 28, 2026, https://bonafurtuna.com/blogs/food-for-thought/how-to-taste-olive-oil-like-a-pro?_pos=1&_sid=9e49422ca&_ss=r.
2. "How to Taste Olive Oil Like a Pro."
3. Maria Lisa Clodoveo, et al., "In the ancient world, virgin olive oil was called 'liquid gold' by Homer and 'the great healer' by Hippocrates. Why has this mythic image been forgotten?," Food Research International 62 (2014): 1062 –1068. https://doi.org/10.1016/j.foodres.2014.05.034.
4. *Merriam-Webster Dictionary*, "tangible," last updated January 25, 2026, https://www.merriam-webster.com/dictionary/tangible.
5. J. W. Simpson Jr., "Spiritual," in *The International Standard Bible Encyclopedia*, rev. ed., Geoffrey W. Bromiley, ed., (Eerdmans, 1979 –1988).

WEEK 5 Day 1

1. "These are the oldest olive trees in the world," Finca Hermosa Nursery, accessed January 28, 2026, https://fincahermosa.com/hermosa/en/oldest-olive-trees-the-world/.
2. "The oldest olive tree in the World!," Mia Elia, June 12, 2020, https://www.miaelia.com/the-oldest-olive-tree-in-the-world/.
3. "These are the oldest olive trees in the world," Finca Hermosa.
4. "These are the oldest olive trees in the world," Finca Hermosa.
5. Alyson Maticic, "Why Is My Olive Tree Dying? [And What to Do About It]," Garden Tabs, accessed January 28, 2026, https://gardentabs.com/why-olive-tree-dying-what-to-do/.
6. Noah Agles, "How To Tell If Olive Tree Is Dead [And How To Revive It]," Garden Tabs, accessed January 28, 2026, https://gardentabs.com/olive-tree-dead/.
7. Sarah Fielding, "Languishing Is the Mood of 2021. How to Identify It and How to Cope," Verywell Mind, last updated September 29, 2021, https://www.verywellmind.com/languishing-is-the-mood-of-2021-5180999.
8. *Merriam-Webster Dictionary*, "flourishing," last updated January 9, 2026, https://www.merriam-webster.com/dictionary/flourishing.
9. Maticic, "Why Is My Olive Tree Dying?."
10. *Merriam-Webster Dictionary*, "languish," last updated January 22, 2026, https://www.merriam-webster.com/dictionary/languish#:~:text=%3A%20to%20be%20or%20become%20feeble,%3A%20to%20become%20dispirited.
11. Fielding, "Languishing Is the Mood of 2021."
12. Sean Buono, "Breaking Through Spiritual Languish," *Focusing on Jesus* (blog), April 22, 2021, http://www.seanbuono.com/2021/04/breaking-through-spiritual-languish.html.
13. Maticic, "Why Is My Olive Tree Dying?."

WEEK 5 Day 2

1. *Holman Illustrated Bible Dictionary*, Chad Brand et al., eds., (Holman Bible Publishers, 2003), under "Heart."

WEEK 5 Day 3

1. Bible Hub, "3340. metanoeó," accessed January 28, 2026, https://biblehub.com/greek/3340.htm.

2. *Oxford English Dictionary*, "renew," last updated December 2025, https://www.oed.com/dictionary/renew_v1?tab=meaning_and_use#26069435.

3. Bible Hub, "5426. phroneó," accessed January 28, 2026, https://biblehub.com/greek/5426.htm.

4. *Merriam-Webster Dictionary*, "mindset," last updated January 23, 2026, https://www.merriam-webster.com/dictionary/mindset.

5. *Bible Sense Lexicon*, Logos Bible Software, 2009, under "true."

6. *Bible Sense Lexicon*, Logos Bible Software, 2009, under "honorable."

7. The summary definitions in the list are based on an assortment of sources. See Ethelbert W. Bullinger, *A Critical Lexicon and Concordance to the English and Greek New Testament* (Longmans, Green, & Co., 1908); *Bible Sense Lexicon*, Logos Bible Software, 2009; John R. Carter, *The Transformed Life: Discover How to Live from the Inside Out* (Harrison House, 2014); James Strong, *A Concise Dictionary of the Words in the Greek Testament and The Hebrew Bible*, Logos Bible Software, 2009; *Merriam-Webster Dictionary*, https://www.merriam-webster.com.

8. Max Lucado, "Strongholds," Max Lucado, September 2015, https://maxlucado.com/strongholds/.

9. E. W. Smith, "Stronghold," in *The International Standard Bible Encyclopedia*, rev. ed., Geoffrey W. Bromiley, ed., (Eerdmans, 1979–1988).

WEEK 5 Day 4

1. "15 Facts About the Human Body!," National Geographic Kids, accessed January 28, 2026, https://www.natgeokids.com/uk/discover/science/general-science/15-facts-about-the-human-body/.

2. "90 Weird & Fun Facts About The Human Body," Nectar, March 16, 2022, https://www.nectarsleep.com/posts/fun-facts-about-the-human-body/.

3. "10 Amazing Facts About the Human Body," Orthopaedic Specialty Group, August 6, 2015, https://www.osgpc.com/amazing-facts-about-the-human-body/.

4. "10 Amazing Facts About the Human Body."

5. "15 Facts About the Human Body!"

6. "10 Amazing Facts About the Human Body."

7. "90 Weird & Fun Facts About The Human Body."

8. "10 Amazing Facts About the Human Body."

9. "15 Facts About the Human Body!"

10. "90 Weird & Fun Facts About The Human Body."

11. "90 Weird & Fun Facts About The Human Body."

12. "15 Facts About the Human Body!"

13. D. M. Gurtner and N. Perrin, "Temple," in *Dictionary of Jesus and the Gospels*, 2nd ed., Joel B. Green, et al., eds., (IVP Academic, 2013).

14. *Bible Sense Lexicon*, Logos Bible Software, 2009, under "to be permissible."

15. *Bible Sense Lexicon*, Logos Bible Software, 2009, under "useful; beneficial."

16. *Bible Sense Lexicon*, Logos Bible Software, 2009, under "to honor ⇔ glorify."

17. Bible Tools, "Strong's #1392: doxazo (pronounced dox-ad'-zo)," accessed January 28, 2026, https://www.bibletools.org/index.cfm/fuseaction/Lexicon.show/ID/G1392/doxazo.htm.

18. Bible Hub, "1391. doxa," accessed January 28, 2026, https://biblehub.com/greek/1391.htm.

WEEK 5 Day 5

1. Olivia Walters, "11 Benefits of a Strong Core," Healthline, last updated March 7, 2022, https://www.healthline.com/health/corestrength-more-important-than-muscular-arms.

2. Walters, "11 Benefits of a Strong Core."

WEEK 6 Day 1

1. Debi Holland, "How to prune olive trees - the best ways and when to prune," Homes & Gardens, May 27, 2002, https://www.homesandgardens.com/gardens/how-to-prune-olive-trees.

2. "How to Prune Olive Trees: A Guide for Pruning Olive Trees," Olives Unlimited, accessed January 28, 2026, https://olivesunlimited.com/how-to-prune-olive-trees/.

3. Holland, "How to prune olive trees."

4. James Strong, *A Concise Dictionary of the Words in the Greek Testament and The Hebrew Bible*, Logos Bible Software, 2009, under "kathairō."

5. *Bible Sense Lexicon*, Logos Bible Software, 2009, under "to prune."

6. *Merriam-Webster Dictionary*, "prune," last updated January 23, 2026, https://www.merriam-webster.com/dictionary/prune.

WEEK 6 Day 2

1. Michele Meleen, "How Long Is a Generation? Today and In History," YourDictionary, last updated June 2, 2020, https://reference.yourdictionary.com/resources/how-long-is-a-generation-todayand-in-history.html.

WEEK 6 Day 3

1. *Dictionary of Bible Themes* (Martin Manser, 2009), under "8260, generosity."

2. R. J. Hughes III, "Generosity; Generous," in *The International Standard Bible Encyclopedia*, rev. ed., Geoffrey W. Bromiley, ed., (Eerdmans, 1979–1988).

3. Hughes III, "Generosity; Generous."

4. Blue Letter Bible, "Lexicon:: Strong's G841 - autarkeia," accessed January 28, 2026, https://www.blueletterbible.org/lexicon/g841/kjv/tr/0-1/.

5. Scott LaPierre, host, *Scott LaPierre Ministries*, podcast, "God Loves a Cheerful Giver and Six Ways to Become One (2 Corinthians 9:7)," Scott LaPierre Ministries, October 20, 2024, https://www.scottlapierre.org/god-loves-a-cheerful-giver/6.

WEEK 6 Day 4

1. The information in this section can be found from the following sources: "Olive Fruit Fly," University of California Statewide IPM Program, last updated October 14, 2026, https://ipm.ucanr.edu/agriculture/olive/olive-fruit-fly/; "Olive Fly Control," The Olive Oil Source, accessed January 28, 2026, https://www.oliveoilsource.com/page/olive-fly-control; "How to Manage Olive Fruit Fly Infestations," Olives Unlimited, accessed January 28, 2026, https://olivesunlimited.com/how-to-manage-olive-fruit-fly-infestations/.

Your Recipes

Use the following pages to collect new or favorite recipes using olives or olive oil.

For inspiration, visit **temeculaoliveoil.com/recipes.**

These recipes have been curated by our friends at the ranch where the videos were recorded. This is a great way to ensure you have a well-rounded feast with various delicious options!

- Appetizers
- Soups
- Salads
- Marinades/Sauces/Dressings
- Sides
- Pasta
- Main Courses
- Desserts
- Vegan/Vegetarian

Start by writing down what you'll bring for the group on Week 7. On the following page, add recipes from group members (or from the website above) that you want to add to your collection. After Week 7, consider sending a group email for each member to reply with the recipe they brought to share.